How to Bake
for Beginners

oven conversions

°C		GAS
140°C	=	1
150°C	=	2
170°C	=	3
180°C	=	4
190°C	=	5
200°C	=	6
220°C	=	7
230°C	=	8
240°C	=	9.

MAHY ELAMIN

How to Bake for BEGINNERS

An Easy Cookbook for Baking the Basics

ROCKRIDGE
PRESS

For general information on our other products and services or to obtain technical support, please contact our Customer Care Department within the United States at (866) 744-2665, or outside the United States at (510) 253-0500.

Rockridge Press publishes its books in a variety of electronic and print formats. Some content that appears in print may not be available in electronic books, and vice versa.

Interior and Cover Designer: Heather Krakora
Art Producer: Sue Bischofberger
Editor: Lauren Ladoceour
Production Editor: Mia Moran

Illustration © Tom Bingham

Photography © Helene Dujardin, pp. xii, 14, 20, 21, 22, 23, 24, 80, 111, 130, 133; © Evi Abeler, pp. 17, 44, 94, 140; © Linda Schneider, p. 30; © Nadine Greeff, pp. 34, 42, 48, 52, 64, 76, 88, 104; © Michele Olivier, p. 38; © Marija Vidal, pp. 58, 82, 134, 152; © Jennifer Davick, pp. 70, 84; © Tara Donne, p. 98; © Happy Hirtzel/Shutterstock, p. 104; © Darren Muir, p. 116; © Lisa Huff, p. 122; © Gillian Vann/Stocksy, p. 126; © Kathariena/iStock, p. 144

Author photo courtesy of Maha Kalache

ISBN: Print 978-1-64611-007-0 | eBook 978-1-64611-008-7

R0

To my girls, Dania and Jana,
who took my baking joy to a whole other level.

Contents

Introduction

I lived in Paris when I was a kid, and I remember feeling mesmerized by the beautiful pastry shops there. My mind was interested, inspired, and intrigued. But I grew up in a busy diplomatic home where I wasn't allowed in the kitchen.

Still, I'd sneak in and watch the chefs and bakers prepare elegant seated dinners and extravagant baked goods. I would watch, feeling like I somehow belonged there, but I would get called away to study. So it wasn't until I left my parents' house that I started cooking and baking.

Going into college I was lost—I couldn't find a single major that interested me. I let a few family friends guide me toward a pharmacy degree. I still don't know how those five years in school (and then another two working in the field) passed by.

All I know is, one day I quit my job—and went into the kitchen to bake some peanut butter cookies. I sat down with a cup of coffee and my cookies, and I broke the news to my husband. I've never felt freer than in that moment.

Those stunning French pastry shop displays had created in me a passion for baking. And, so, with time on my hands, I started baking from scratch. Although I'd read books on baking and tried to understand the fundamentals, I basically just dove right in. I laugh now because I naively believed I could instantly create whatever fancy dessert I desired. It was definitely fun trying to bake, but it was no fun having failure after failure. My first tiramisu, for example, was a total disaster because I didn't even know how to separate eggs properly.

The tiramisu came out nothing like what I had in mind, but that was when I realized I needed to start simply. I began with a classic white cake. I wanted to achieve fluffy white cake perfection before moving on. I then learned to whip cream, and once I honed that skill, I added espresso. Eventually, I layered my perfect white cake with espresso whipped cream and dusted it with cocoa powder. It was not exactly tiramisu, but it was the best thing I ever had.

Finally, I turned to my science background for help. I wanted to understand why certain recipes worked but others didn't. Even more, I wanted to understand why certain recipes are good, but others are terrific! I dove deep into understanding the structure, chemical reactions, composition, and formulation of every recipe. The more I understood the baking process, the more I experimented, the more success I had, the more joy it brought to my life—and the more addicted to it I became. I couldn't stop. I was baking something new every single day.

About 10 years ago, I turned my baking obsession into a career. I now teach other people who are brand-new to the kitchen, the way I once was. Baking can be so mystifying when you're experimenting on your own at home, as I did when I first quit my life as a pharmacist. That's why I've put together this book of essential tools and techniques, along with easy foolproof recipes, to get you started on your own baking path—one you'll quickly come to love.

All of the recipes here are forgiving in their technique, which means you'll be hard-pressed to mess them up. My hope is that as you get more experience, you'll gain more confidence and, in the process, discover the joy and satisfaction of creating a delicious, decadent masterpiece out of simple ingredients.

Throughout this book, I'll teach you the basics that are often assumed—things such as why it's important to use specific ingredients, like baking powder, and how to perform foundational baking techniques, like creaming. You'll learn how to make a perfectly flaky piecrust without a food processor, a delicious breakfast cookie, your friend's favorite birthday cake, the pie you crave every holiday season, a hearty bread to go with your soup—and even how to re-create that muffin you used to buy every morning at the coffee shop. As you read this book and try the recipes, things will connect and your baking skills will grow.

Baking has brightened my life, and I hope this book brings you the joy, happiness, and love baking offers.

PART ONE

Getting Started

CHAPTER ONE

Welcome to the World of Baking

You might have heard that baking is an exact science and not to be taken lightly. The truth is that baking is a joy like no other. To begin, let's discuss basic ingredients and tools, then move on to fundamental culinary definitions and troubleshooting.

Baking Versus Cooking

Both baking and cooking involve heat (direct, indirect, or both) to transform ingredients into a finished dish or treat.

Each has room for creativity, but on a very different scale. When cooking, you can swap types of proteins or veggies, increase salt, and add flavor enhancers, such as lemon juice, even if it's not in the recipe, and your results will not suffer.

When baking, you can swap fruit, nuts, and even chocolates. But adding lemon juice to a cake batter that requires a neutral level of acidity can result in something very different than what you were expecting. That's why good recipes are important. If you follow the recipe as written, you'll end up with a warm treat and a home that smells like a bakery. To make life easier, many recipes in this book include variations so you'll know exactly what's okay to substitute and what's not.

A Baker's Dozen Keys to Success

1 Bake for the love of it! This isn't a chore—it shouldn't feel like one.

2 Don't rush. Plan your time and use every minute to enjoy the process and let the smells of baked goods fill your home.

3 Read the entire recipe before you begin. Imagine the steps so, when you start the baking process, it will feel familiar.

4 Make sure you have all the ingredients and the correct baking pan(s) on hand. (Another great reason to read the recipe first!)

5 Pay attention to the baking temperature and to the ingredients, both types and amounts.

6 Use the best-quality ingredients you can afford. If you use a bad-tasting chocolate bar for a chocolate cake, you'll end up with that same bad taste in your cake.

7 Look for texture cues in recipes, such as to leave lumps in a batter or to mix until silky smooth. These affect the results.

8 Clean as you go (especially during baking times).

9 Your oven is your best friend. As you bake, observe areas that create quicker browning. Based on that, rotate your pans and adjust oven racks so the food bakes more evenly.

10 Always preheat the oven. Placing a batter or dough in a cool oven can ruin any chances of ingredients dissolving together, leavening, and getting the crust and texture you want.

11 Check for doneness before you turn off the oven or let something cool.

12 Share! Baking is a wonderful family activity and a great way to fundraise for your favorite charities or to welcome new neighbors.

13 Bake with confidence. Despite its formulas, baking is forgiving. Embrace your mistakes as valuable, and sometimes still delicious, lessons.

Essential Ingredients

There are lots of ingredients in the baking aisles. To help you decide what you need, I've made a list of essential ingredients with some information on how to best understand and use each of them. Let's break them down into pantry and refrigerator categories to make things easier.

IN THE PANTRY

Baking powder: This ingredient is a leavener, which is a substance used in dough or a batter to make it rise. Baking with the correct type of leavener, meaning the type specified in the recipe, is crucial for proper results. Recipes in this book require double-acting baking powder, and I always use an aluminum-free product, which ensures no metallic aftertaste in the finished baked good.

Baking soda: Like baking powder, baking soda is a leavener responsible for making baked goods rise. Do not ever swap baking soda for baking powder. Although they both make baked goods rise, baking soda and baking powder are not the same ingredient and each produces a different chemical reaction based on the ingredients with which it is combined!

Butter: For baking purposes, use unsalted butter so you control the total amount of salt in your recipe. The temperature of the butter specified in the recipe is important for baking success. Butter reacts differently in baking when it is frozen versus room temperature versus melted.

➢ Frozen butter creates a flaky texture, so it is ideal in pie doughs.

➢ Room-temperature butter creates a beautiful airy texture in cakes and produces perfect cookie dough.

➢ Melted butter adds lots of moisture to muffins and cakes, which produces a denser texture.

Chocolate: When you melt or shave chocolate, reach for baking chocolate or chocolate bars. Save chocolate chips for suspending in cakes and batters, or for garnishing. The main types of chocolate are dark, semisweet, and milk. You can use them interchangeably to suit your taste.

Cocoa powder: There are two main types—natural and Dutch process cocoa powder, which is processed to be less acidic than natural cocoa powder. Dutch process has a deeper, richer chocolate taste and a darker color. The two types can be used interchangeably, but the result will be slightly darker in color and taste less acidic when using Dutch process cocoa powder.

Dried fruits and nuts: The recipes in this book most often use dried apricots, cranberries, and raisins, as well as hazelnuts, pecans, walnuts, and coconut.

Flour: Obviously, flour is a very important ingredient in baking. It builds structure, shape, and texture. Cake flour ensures a delicate crumb—a more fragile texture—whereas bread flour offers a chewy texture for pizza crust and bread loaves. All-purpose flour works for every baked good, so most recipes in this book call for all-purpose flour. Occasionally cake flour, whole-wheat flour, or a nut flour are specified.

Oats: Oats add a nutty flavor and texture to cookies and bars. For baking, stock up on old-fashioned rolled oats or quick-cooking oats—not the steel-cut variety, which can result in an unpleasant texture.

Oil: Use a neutral-tasting oil, such as sunflower, canola, light olive oil, or corn, because neutral oils will not affect the flavor or smell of any baked goods. Something stronger, like extra-virgin olive oil, will have a distinct aroma and taste if added to a batter.

Salt: Salt enhances flavor in both cooking and baking—yes, baking. Salt perks up chocolate's deep flavor and highlights sugar's sweetness. I recommend using pink Himalayan salt or kosher salt, not table salt, which tastes too "salty" and has added preservatives and iodine.

Spices: Among the ground spices used in baking, ground cinnamon probably tops the list, along with ginger, nutmeg, and cardamom.

Sugar: Granulated sugar is the most common type used for batters and doughs, and confectioners' sugar is great for icing and dusting. Coarser types, such as demerara and sanding sugars, are nice for garnishing baked goods and lending a sweet finishing crunch, and brown sugar adds extra moisture and a nutty flavor.

Vanilla extract: Vanilla extract provides the vanilla flavor you expect, and enhances and enriches other flavors in your baked goods. A little goes a long way—in most recipes only a teaspoon is needed. Always buy real vanilla extract, not imitation. Your taste buds will thank you.

IN THE REFRIGERATOR

Dairy: Milk, yogurt, sour cream, heavy (whipping) cream, and cream cheese add that desirably moist mouthfeel to cakes, muffins, and breads. They also help increase browning, enrich flavor, and create a fine crumb.

Eggs: As a rule of thumb, whenever an egg is used in a recipe, use a large egg.

Yeast: Yeast is a type of fungus that, once activated, expands breads and doughs by creating air bubbles and emitting gas. It is best kept in the freezer, where it can remain for years. By freezing yeast, you keep it inactive until it's time to use it. For more information on the types of yeast and how to activate yeast, see page 131.

Essential Gear

These essential tools and equipment are simple, yet will make the baking process much smoother and more efficient!

KITCHEN TOOLS

Bowls: You should have stainless steel, ceramic, or plastic bowls of different sizes—small, medium, and large to start—for mixing batters, crusts, frostings, fillings, and more.

Fine-mesh sieve: At a minimum, buy a large sieve for sifting flour or dusting confectioners' sugar.

Ice cream scoop: This is handy for dividing cookie dough and filling muffin pans. If you don't have one, you can use a spoon or measuring cup, depending on the amounts needed.

Knives: A chef's knife is essential for chopping chocolate and nuts or cutting out biscuit dough. A serrated knife easily cuts baked bread, and a paring knife will make precise work of trimming and dicing fruit or of scoring dough.

Liners: Lining your pans with a nonstick paper, such as parchment paper, or reusable silicone baking mats means no sticky surprises and makes cleanup a breeze.

Measuring cups and spoons: These usually come as nested sets and are inexpensive items you will use every time you bake. Typical measures include 1 cup, ½ cup, ⅓ cup, ¼ cup, 1 tablespoon, 1 teaspoon, ½ teaspoon, and ¼ teaspoon.

Pastry brush: You'll use this pastry brush to brush butter on breads and muffins, grease baking pans and molds, and glaze cake layers.

Rolling pin: Start with a wooden or marble rolling pin with an even diameter and short handles on the ends. As you gain experience, you'll want to move on to French-style rolling pins. A French pin is thinner in diameter than a regular rolling pin and has no handles—it's basically a wooden cylinder that narrows toward the ends. The French-style pins give you more control over the dough.

Rubber spatula: This tool helps you get every bit of batter or dough out of your bowls and is useful when folding ingredients together. You'll learn more about folding on page 23.

Whisk: This simple wire tool blends dry ingredients evenly and mixes wet ingredients into a smooth batter. I prefer a whisk and rubber spatula to a wooden spoon. The whisk offers better blending with less effort; likewise, the spatula will more cleanly scrape a bowl.

Wooden spoon: A classic tool used to blend quick bread, muffin, and even brownie batters. If this is your preferred mixing tool, keep one designated just for baking so it doesn't pick up any onion, garlic, or harsh spice flavors you don't want in your baked goods!

Zester or grater: You'll need a tool, such as a box grater or a Microplane, to zest citrus and to grate chocolate and frozen butter.

BAKING EQUIPMENT

Baking pans, baking sheets, and sheet pans: You'll want a 12-cup muffin pan, a 24-cup mini-muffin pan, square baking pans, round cake pans, a few baking sheets, a loaf pan, a pie pan, a tart pan, and a rimmed sheet pan.

Handheld electric mixer: A hand mixer is great for creaming, whipping, mixing, and much more! It is a workhorse in the baker's kitchen.

Oven mitts: These insulated heat-resistant gloves help you get a firm, safe grip on your hot baking pans and sheets.

Stovetop pots and pans: Some recipes include cooking down a fruit, warming honey, or melting butter before adding them to your batter.

Wire cooling racks: Placing baked items on these racks will allow air to circulate around your baked goods in a way that prevents sogginess and allows faster cooling.

KEY CUTS

While baking, you may find yourself reaching for a knife more often than you expect. Make sure you use the correct knife for every task. A chef's knife is a great tool to chop chocolate or nuts. Serrated knives cleanly cut through cakes and breads. A smaller paring knife is great for slicing strawberries, peaches, and other fruits or decorative components.

Choose very sharp knives. Although a dull knife may seem safer, sharp knives are in fact safer to use because sharp knives require minimal force to cut, and the object you're cutting won't slip and slide under excess pressure, which is the main cause of knife accidents.

PROPER GRIP

The most efficient and safest way to master knife skills is to hold your knife properly. There are two parts to a knife: the handle and the blade. To hold a knife properly, place your hand entirely on the handle and grip it firmly. Practice rocking the knife blade back and forth while maintaining a firm grip on the handle.

ROUGH CHOPPING NUTS

Group together the nuts to be chopped on the cutting board. Place one hand entirely on the knife handle and grip it firmly. Place your other hand over the top of the knife and use it to push down as you rock the knife up and down over the nuts.

SLICING FRUIT

A small paring knife is best for slicing fruits. Working on a cutting board, hold the fruit in place with your nondominant hand. Use your other hand to firmly grip the knife handle and gently cut slices, as desired.

ZESTING CITRUS

A Microplane is my favorite tool for zesting citrus. It's a sharp rasp-like tool. You run your citrus, or other food to be grated or zested, over the tool's tiny blades until the colored part of the peel is grated off. Stop when you see the white pith underneath, because it's bitter. You can also use this tool on chocolate and butter.

Cooking with Heat

Baking involves the transfer of heat by conduction, convection, induction, or radiant heat. The types of heat are all used differently.

Conduction cooking is a slower process of heat transfer from one molecule to another through direct contact, which is how stovetop cooking occurs. Heat is conducted to the food through a skillet or pot.

Convection cooking is a heat transfer using a fan to circulate the air (or gas or steam) around the food. Many ovens have a fan for convection baking, which is a faster way to bake and cook.

Induction cooking is a form of heat transfer through magnetic fields. Induction heating is mostly used for stovetop cooking, and it's very fast compared with conduction or other forms of heat transfer.

Radiant heat cooking is basically a rapid transfer of heat from a warmer object to a cooler one. Conventional ovens use radiant heat for baking.

STOVETOP SUCCESS

· Keep all pot and pan handles facing in, so you don't accidentally bump into them and spill hot ingredients all over your kitchen or yourself.

· Always use a larger pot than you think is necessary. You may have to whisk or stir the mixture, which will spill if the pan is too small.

· Avoid using wooden spoons or any utensils with wooden handles because they may burn.

· Avoid placing a small pot on a large burner. Always make sure the bottom of the pot is the same size or larger than the burner, which helps prevent burning and makes heat use and cooking more efficient.

· Do not leave a saucepan or skillet unattended on the stove as it may heat up faster than you think and create a fire hazard.

· Oil and alcohol may spark fire immediately if they come in contact with direct heat, so be extra careful when using either ingredient.

· Tie back your hair and roll up your sleeves when using the stove.

FIRE, BLADES, AND GERMS

The kitchen is a source of joy, and there are precautions to take to ensure that the experience remains joyful.

> **Kitchen fires: Although kitchen fires aren't uncommon, thankfully they're easily preventable.** Do not leave an empty pot or skillet on the hot stove unattended, and don't forget to turn off the oven or a burner. Also never use a parchment paper–lined baking sheet under the broiler. Keep a multipurpose fire extinguisher on hand, just in case.

> **Sharp stuff: Knives, graters, and peelers can be your best friends in the kitchen and will serve you long and well if used and cared for properly.** However, they all have sharp blades, so always maintain a firm, proper, and safe grip on them.

> **Bacteria: Cross-contamination is common in many busy kitchens.** Some simple precautions include making sure your kitchen counters are well cleaned before starting the baking process, and washing and drying all fresh fruit before you use it. Even lemons and oranges should be washed before zesting.

The heat in your oven will kill any germs present in raw batters, but once baked goods have cooled, you should store them properly to avoid allowing them to develop any bacteria (see storage guidelines for each chapter). This applies especially to cakes, fruit-based goods, and anything with cream or dairy.

The oven is like the sous chef for bakers, so understanding how to use it and keeping it in good shape are crucial to your baking success.

· Inspect your oven's heating elements and make sure your oven door locks properly. If your oven is electric, the heating elements should be red and uniform in color. If your oven is gas, make sure the heat is uniform on both sides. Also, make sure the heating elements are not cracked and are not covered in baked food spills that might block the heat.

· Keep your oven clean. If you have a self-cleaning oven function, use it. Otherwise, wipe away any burnt foods or grease stains in your oven before using it again.

· If the recipe indicates a specific position for your oven rack, position the rack(s) before preheating the oven.

· Preheating the oven is the first step in the baking process. This is important so your batters don't have to sit before baking, which may affect the efficiency of certain ingredients such as baking powder. It also ensures a proper cooking temperature and time.

· Make sure your oven light is working so you can check the progress without opening the oven door and losing precious cooking heat.

How to Use a Recipe

Before you start baking, review the recipe to determine if it requires any special equipment or tools, to find out the total time you'll need, and how many servings the recipe makes. Then, read the ingredients list and make sure you have everything on hand.

Next, review the numbered instructions and visualize them in your mind— see yourself making the recipe step by step. Trust me: This will pay off later as you begin the actual baking process. It will feel familiar, easy, and as though you've done it before!

Finally, read the tips and variations. Maybe you'll want to substitute one ingredient for another. Maybe you'll want to prepare a few steps in advance or make the recipe ahead to bake another day. These tips and variations help you plan the baking process and help you personalize everything you bake to your taste.

BAKING LINGO

Beat: Mix the ingredients, usually at a higher speed, to soften them. As a rule of thumb, when whipping or beating anything, always start on the lowest speed and gradually work up to the highest speed within 1 minute. Continue beating on the highest speed for the remainder of the recipe.

Blend: Mix together at least two different ingredients until they become a single element.

Chop: Cut an ingredient using a knife or food processor.

Combine: Bring different ingredients together with minimal mixing.

Cool: Let the oven heat dissipate until the baked goods reach room temperature.

Cream: Beat butter until it turns pale yellow and becomes fluffy in texture. This can be done with just butter or with a combination of butter and sugar.

Cut in: Blend a type of fat, usually butter, into a type of flour without beating or creaming the butter.

Dissolve: Blend a solid into a liquid until the solids no longer appear in the liquid solution, such as dissolving salt in water or sugar in water.

Dot: Drop bits and pieces randomly, for example dotting butter over a pie filling.

Dry ingredients: Ingredients that contain no liquid, such as flour, leavening agents, cocoa powder, sugar, and salt. Dry ingredients are best blended together before being added to any liquid ingredients. These ingredients are best measured using measuring cups and spoons (see page 17).

Dust: Lightly sprinkle a dry ingredient, flour or sugar for example, on either a work surface or a baked good.

Egg wash: Beat an egg with a small amount of liquid (water, cream, or milk), then brush it on unbaked pastries or breads to provide a sheen or to help in browning.

Flour: Coat a greased baking pan with a dusting of flour, or sprinkle flour on a work surface before rolling out dough.

Fold: Gently mix certain ingredients, usually already whipped, with a rubber spatula using a gentle up-and-down circular motion around the whole bowl. This is used to incorporate whipped egg whites into a dense batter, for example, to help preserve the air you've worked so hard to incorporate into your batter or other ingredients.

Garnish: Add an ingredient to a finished baked product, whether for taste, texture, or visual appeal.

Grease: Add a thin layer of fat (butter or oil) to a baking pan.

Knead: Use the heel of your hand to fold dough into quarter folds with a rotation after every fold.

Leavening: This process of gas release during baking creates an airy, risen texture in your baked goods. Yeast, baking soda, and baking powder are examples of leavening agents.

Melt: Use heat to liquefy ingredients.

Pit: Remove pits from fruits.

Preheat: Heat your oven to the desired recipe temperature before placing your filled pan in the oven.

Proof: Let a yeast dough rest at room temperature and double in size as it releases the gases produced by the yeast.

Scald: Heat milk to just below its boiling point.

Sift: Pass a dry ingredient, such as flour, cornstarch, leavening agents, or sugar, through a fine-mesh sieve to separate any lumps and process it into finer particles. This ensures uniform baking.

Simmer: Heat liquids to just below their boiling point. Tiny bubbles should appear only around the edges and never in the center of the liquid being simmered.

Sprinkle: Scatter tiny pieces of ingredients over a surface.

Stir: Mix ingredients in a circular motion to blend or combine them, usually with a spoon.

Toss: Gently mix ingredients, usually incorporating larger particles.

Wet ingredients: These ingredients contain liquid. Examples are eggs, fats (oil or butter), dairy products, juices, liquid extracts, and sugars and sweeteners. Although not physically a liquid, in baking, sugar is most often mixed with a liquid so it can properly do its job, so it is classified as a liquid. Use a liquid measuring cup (see page 18) to measure liquids.

Whip: Vigorously mix an ingredient to incorporate air until the ingredient has tripled in volume, usually for whipping cream or egg whites.

Yield: This is the amount of baked goods you'll end up with after completing the recipe.

Zest: Extract the outer peel of a citrus for flavoring.

CHAPTER TWO

Fundamental Skills

Now that you've learned about essential kitchen tools and baking equipment—and mastered the lingo—let's move on to basic baking skills. These skills are used in most of the recipes in this book. Proficiency in these basic baking skills will help you bake with confidence. The beauty of these skills is that they form the foundation of your learning—and get easier with practice.

Once you've completed this chapter, you'll be ready to put your new skills to work. Armed with your new knowledge and my foolproof recipes, you'll be a baking pro in no time!

Prepping Pans

Select the right size pans for your recipe, and prepare them to keep your baked goods from sticking. Start with clean pans. Make sure they're not scratched or rusted and don't have any remaining bits of baked goods on them. Line your pans with baking paper, parchment paper, or a silicone baking mat. This guarantees no sticking, and your pan will be easier to clean. In some cases, you'll need to coat the pan with a thin layer of butter or oil, which is easily done using a pastry brush.

Handling Eggs

GETTING EGGS TO THE CORRECT TEMPERATURE

Eggs are a magical ingredient in baking. They create structure in baked goods, they add moisture and create a tender texture, and they bind the dry ingredients to the wet ingredients in batters. For eggs to work their magic, however, they need to be at room temperature before being incorporated into your recipes (unless, of course, a recipe states otherwise).

You should always keep eggs refrigerated until needed. Simply remove the eggs from the refrigerator about 1 hour before you start baking so they can reach room temperature. However, do not leave raw eggs unrefrigerated for more than 2 hours, and always avoid consuming raw eggs. If you're in a hurry or if you forgot to take them out of the refrigerator in advance, place the cold eggs in a bowl of warm (not hot) water for about 5 minutes to warm them to room temperature.

CRACKING EGGS

People variously crack their eggs on the rim of a bowl, using a knife, or by banging two eggs against each other. Although these techniques work, you'll most likely end up with bits of shell in your bowl when cracking eggs in these ways. My favorite way to crack an egg? Tap the egg on a flat surface in a quick decisive motion. Then, use your two thumbs and index fingers to break the shell into two pieces. Clean up any spills immediately.

SEPARATING EGGS

In recipes, sometimes just the white or just the yolk is required. Egg yolks and whites act differently in baking recipes. Egg yolks provide richness while egg whites provide a fluffy, airy texture.

To separate the egg yolk from the white, simply crack the egg and let the yolk rest in one part of the shell while allowing the egg white to slip into a bowl below. Or gently crack the egg and pour it over a large slotted spoon placed over a bowl. The egg white should pass through the slotted spoon, leaving only the yolk on the spoon. You may need to shake the spoon lightly to help all the egg white pass through. My favorite technique, however, is to separate eggs using

just my hands. It's a bit of an advanced technique, but go ahead and try it, if you dare. It's not really that difficult once you get the hang of it! Crack the egg with one hand and pour it all into the other hand held over a bowl. Let the egg whites pass through your fingers into the bowl below.

To avoid waste, if your recipe calls for just one part of the egg, refrigerate the remaining part in an airtight container and use it in another recipe, such as for an omelet, within 2 to 4 days.

Measuring Ingredients

Recipes include the necessary amounts of all the ingredients, and learning how to measure those ingredients properly is the first class in Baking 101. Using the correct ingredients in the correct amounts is a foolproof way to guarantee your recipe's success. There are specific measuring tools and techniques to help you get the best results.

Dry ingredients (such as sugar and flour) are best quantified using measuring cups and spoons. They come in amounts as big as 1 cup and as small as ⅛ of a teaspoon and everything in between.

Liquid measuring cups, for measuring liquid ingredients such as milk or water, are larger—usually 1 to 4 cups in capacity—and made of clear glass or plastic. A liquid measuring cup has its volume increments marked on the side of the glass and usually features a spout to make pouring the ingredients easier and less messy. You just add the ingredient you're measuring until it reaches the desired mark. Although it may be tempting to measure liquids in a dry measuring cup, chances are you won't be able to fill it to the top and transfer it to the bowl without spilling—meaning your measurement will not be accurate. However, for smaller amounts, such as teaspoons and tablespoons, you can use the same nested measuring spoons used for dry ingredients.

Melting

Melting is a baking process that turns a solid ingredient into a liquid state. The most common ingredients that bakers melt are butter and chocolate. A classic melting method involves a double boiler, which is created by placing a heatproof bowl or double boiler insert over a pot of simmering water. The bowl should fit over the pot so it doesn't touch the simmering water. The butter or chocolate is then added to the bowl. As it's stirred, it will melt slowly from the water's heat. These ingredients can also be melted in the microwave for an easier, faster experience.

Melting chocolate in a microwave uses fewer pans and pots than the double boiler technique and takes a fraction of the time. To melt chocolate in a microwave:

· Use a microwave-safe bowl that's about twice the size of the amount of chocolate you need to melt.

- Cut the chocolate into equal-size chunks and place the chunks into the bowl.

- Microwave the chocolate on high power for 30 seconds. Whisk well. If it has not melted, microwave the chocolate again, but this time for 15 seconds. Whisk again. Continue to microwave, as needed, in 15-second increments, whisking in between, until the chocolate melts.

- Always microwave in small intervals and whisk in between. Do not microwave the chocolate until it is completely melted or it may burn.

Butter consists of nearly 20 percent water, so melting it removes the water and changes the structure of the butter. To melt butter in the microwave:

- Cut the butter into tablespoon-size portions and place them into a microwave-safe bowl.

- Microwave the butter on high power for 40 seconds. Remove it and stir the butter until it melts. If it doesn't melt completely, microwave it in 15-second intervals, stirring after each interval until melted.

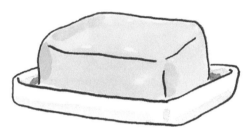

You can also melt butter in a pot directly on the stovetop, but be careful because it can burn very quickly.

> **TIP:** Room-temperature butter is a common element in many recipes. To bring butter to room temperature from the refrigerator, place the cold butter on the counter and let it sit for 30 minutes.

Mixing

In baking, mixing can be quite specific—unlike in cooking. Once you learn the basics, the more you bake the more you'll know intuitively which technique is best for what you're baking.

STIRRING

In baking, this means a constant motion until a desired level of mixing is reached. Stirring can be done over heat or not, and can be done using a whisk, wooden spoon, spatula, fork, or any tool that gives you the desired results.

CREAMING

Creaming usually involves an electric mixer (but can be done with a bowl and wooden spoon). It can take 2 to 4 minutes to beat butter (with or without sugar) until it becomes light and pale in color and takes on a fluffy texture.

CUTTING IN

To cut in, you'll use a knife, fork, pastry cutter, or your fingers to incorporate butter into flour, or a flour mixture, without creaming or softening the butter in any way. You'll be left with pebbles of flour and butter. Recipes will typically note what size pebbles to look for so you don't accidentally overwork the fat.

FOLDING

To fold, use a rubber spatula and a soft, circular, up-and-down motion to ever-so-gently combine ingredients, such as whipped egg whites and batter.

WHIPPING

Whipping is just heavy whisking that incorporates air into your mixture. If you need to incorporate air into an ingredient, use a mixer with a whisk attachment or a whisk in a vigorous mixing motion until you've achieved the desired volume.

HOW TO MAKE WHIPPED CREAM

To make whipped cream, it's easiest to use a handheld electric mixer.

1 **Start by placing 1 cup of cold heavy (whipping) cream into a 1-quart bowl.** Using cold cream is essential for it to whip properly. If you can, chill your bowl ahead of time to make the whipping process easier.

2 **Add 2 tablespoons of confectioners' sugar and 1 teaspoon of vanilla extract to the cream.**

3 **Submerge the beaters into the liquid and hold the rim of the bowl with your other hand.** Begin whipping on low speed for 1 to 2 minutes until you get the feel of it.

4 **Gradually increase the speed while moving the mixer in a light circular motion around the bowl to be sure you're reaching all the ingredients.** Because whipping incorporates air into the cream, you want to make sure the air is incorporated as evenly as possible—that's the reason for the rotation.

5 **Whip the cream for 3 to 4 minutes on medium-high speed, continuing to move the mixer in a circular motion inside the bowl.** Whipped cream is very forgiving, so feel free to stop the whipping process and check how your peaks are forming. Aim for a peak that holds its shape yet is not tough and curdled.

Making Batter

The English word *batter* is derived from the French word *battre*, which means to beat. Although not all batters need heavy beating, they do need some type of whisking and mixing.

Batters are usually loose enough to be poured, like cake, muffin, or pancake batters. Cake batters involve beating the sugar and butter together before adding the remaining ingredients. Muffin or quick bread batter involves whisking wet ingredients separately from dry ingredients and blending them before baking. Although the techniques may be different, the thickness and consistency of both batters are often similar.

Making Dough

Dough in baking can be cookie dough, pastry dough, or bread dough. They're each different in consistency and technique.

COOKIE DOUGH

Basic cookie dough is, well, basic. The simple process usually is as follows:

1   Cream room-temperature butter with sugar for a few minutes.

2   Add eggs to the butter and sugar mixture.

3   In a separate bowl, mix the dry ingredients, and then add the dry ingredients to the wet ingredients little by little, mixing until the dough has formed.

PASTRY DOUGH

Pastry dough has a reputation for being tricky to work with because it involves very cold butter, which needs to be coated in flour yet remain cold during the process. Since beating produces heat, it doesn't work well as a technique for making pastry dough. Pastry dough should be handled minimally.

I've found a foolproof technique to achieve flaky pastry dough, which works the dough as little as possible:

1   **Start by freezing the butter.** Once frozen, use a box grater to grate the frozen butter into mozzarella-like shreds, right into the bowl containing the flour, sugar, and salt.

2   **Using a fork, toss the flour and butter until the flour evenly coats the butter.**

3   **Mix in the ice water and the dough is ready!**

BREAD DOUGH

Making bread dough usually involves a yeast fermentation process. Dissolving the yeast in warm water mixed with sugar allows the yeast to activate and start creating gas. The release of the gas is what expands the bread dough.

Bread doughs are usually firmer to the touch than cookie or pastry doughs. They are kneaded to make them elastic and malleable. This is the basic method for making bread dough:

1   **In a small bowl, stir together the yeast, sugar, and warm liquid (usually water or milk).** Let it sit to activate.

2   **Add the butter, eggs, or oils.**

3   **Add the flour and knead the dough to develop the protein in the flour and make elastic and malleable dough.**

PART TWO

Foolproof Recipes

CHAPTER THREE

Bars

Bars are a fun category in baking because they come in so many varieties. Some bars include a crust; others don't. Bars can be entirely soft, or crunchy, or a mix of crispy on the bottom and creamy on top. But I think the best thing about bars is how easy and delicious they are!

Keys to Baking Bars

· In most bar recipes, you'll notice a two-step baking process: one step for baking the crust and one for baking the filling. Make sure to bake the crust the first time just until it sets—you don't need it to be golden and fully browned because it will be baked again with the filling.

· After you pour the filling (or spread it, depending on how thick the filling is), shake the baking pan slightly to level the filling. This helps spread the filling in an even layer, which promotes even baking. If you notice air bubbles in the filling, lightly tap the pan on the counter to release them.

· Always bake bars on the middle rack of the oven.

· When the bars come out of the oven, they'll be hot and too soft for cutting. So always wait until the bars have cooled for least 30 minutes to cut them into squares or rectangles.

BREAKFAST OATMEAL BARS (PAGE 33)

Checking for Doneness

For the bar recipes in this chapter, you can open the oven door to check them without any risk of ruining the outcome because bars don't contain any leaveners (see page 13). When baking doughs with leaveners, it's important to wait until the baked good has risen properly and its structure has developed before opening the oven and releasing the heat, or it will collapse and will not re-rise. Fortunately, bars don't carry that risk.

Remember: The first bake of the crust is done as soon as it's firm to the touch and slightly golden.

To check the filling for doneness, gently shake the pan. The filling should jiggle very slightly in the center if it was a liquid to begin with. If the filling was more paste-like at the start, it should be completely set when done (no jiggling when shaken).

Storage Guidelines

Different bars have different storage guidelines depending on the type of filling. Generally, if bars contain eggs and dairy then they should be refrigerated. Other bars, however, with a filling based on nuts, butter, sugar, oats, or chocolate, for example, are safe to store on the counter in an airtight container.

To freeze bars, let them cool completely and then wrap each one individually in plastic wrap. Freeze the bars in an airtight container and thaw them on the counter before eating. If desired, you can reheat the bars in a 350°F oven for 3 to 5 minutes after thawing.

Breakfast Oatmeal Bars

These sweet oat-y bars will remind you of your favorite bowl of oatmeal. In fact, they make a perfect breakfast to go!

Makes 16 bars
Prep time: 15 minutes | Bake time: 35 minutes

3 cups old-fashioned **rolled oats**

1¾ cups **milk**

2 large **eggs**

½ cup **honey**

4 tablespoons **unsalted butter**, melted

¼ cup packed **light brown sugar**

1 teaspoon **double-acting baking powder**

1 teaspoon **vanilla extract**

Pinch **salt**

1 cup **raspberries,** fresh or frozen

½ cup **coconut flakes**

½ cup **chocolate chips**

1. Place an oven rack in the middle position and preheat the oven to 350°F. Line the bottom of an 8-inch square baking pan with parchment paper.

2. In a large bowl, whisk the oats, milk, eggs, honey, melted butter, brown sugar, baking powder, vanilla, and salt until combined.

3. Use a spatula to gently fold the raspberries, coconut, and chocolate chips into the batter. Pour the batter into the prepared baking pan.

4. Bake for 35 minutes, or until the oatmeal appears set. Overbaking the bars will result in a dry, chewy bar. Let cool for 15 minutes before cutting into 16 bars.

➤ **Swap it:** If you like the taste of maple, swap in the same amount of maple syrup for the honey. You can replace the raspberries with the same amount of any type of berry. You can even use 1 cup of diced frozen or fresh peaches, apples, or any other fruit. Or sprinkle in 1 teaspoon of ground cinnamon, 1 teaspoon of chai spice, or $1/2$ teaspoon of ground ginger to add a little spice to your morning.

Fudge Brownies with Walnuts

Almost everyone I know has a thing for brownies, especially a rich, fudgy, divine brownie like this one.

Makes 16 brownies
Prep time: 15 minutes | Bake time: 26 minutes

6 tablespoons **unsalted butter**, melted

2 tablespoons **canola oil**

1 cup **sugar**

2 large **eggs**

Pinch **salt**

⅔ cup **cocoa powder**

⅓ cup **all-purpose flour**

½ cup chopped **semisweet chocolate pieces**

½ cup chopped **walnuts**

1. Place an oven rack in the middle position and preheat the oven to 375°F. Line an 8-inch square pan with parchment paper, letting the parchment hang over on two opposite sides of the pan.

2. In a large bowl, whisk the melted butter, canola oil, sugar, eggs, and salt until combined. (The combination of butter and oil here adds extra moistness to the brownies.)

3. Add the cocoa powder and flour. Whisk to blend the batter together.

4. Fold chocolate into the batter. Then use the spatula to scrape the brownie batter into the prepared pan. Top with walnuts.

5. Bake the brownies for 22 to 26 minutes, until they puff slightly. They're done when a toothpick inserted into the center comes out with only a few moist crumbs attached.

6. Remove the pan from the oven. Let the brownies cool in the pan for 5 minutes before using the overhanging parchment as a helper to lift the brownies out. Let cool for at least 30 minutes more before cutting into 16 brownies.

➤ **Beyond the basics:** To punch up the flavor even further, fold 1 cup of coconut flakes into the batter before baking. Or unwrap ½ cup of bite-size caramel cubes and press them into the batter before baking.

Crispy Pecan Pie Bars

Imagine your beloved pecan pie—with a buttery cookie crust and an extra kick from honey in the filling—cut into squares for easy eating!

Makes 16 bars
Prep time: 15 minutes | Bake time: 35 minutes

FOR THE CRUST

¾ cup **unsalted butter**, at room temperature

½ cup packed **light brown sugar**

1¾ cups **all-purpose flour**

⅛ teaspoon **salt**

FOR THE FILLING

⅔ cup packed **light brown sugar**

4 tablespoons **unsalted butter**, at room temperature

¼ cup **honey** (or maple syrup)

2 tablespoons **heavy (whipping) cream**

1 teaspoon **vanilla extract**

1½ cups chopped **pecans**

TO MAKE THE CRUST

1. Place an oven rack in the middle position and preheat the oven to 350°F. Line an 8-inch square baking pan with parchment paper, leaving a 2-inch overhang on all sides.

2. In a large bowl, using a handheld electric mixer, cream the butter and brown sugar for 3 minutes, starting on the lowest speed and gradually increasing to the highest speed, until the mixture is fluffy and light in color. Add the flour and salt. Mix on low speed until the dough looks crumbly. Press the crust firmly into the bottom of the prepared pan with your hands to make sure the bottom is coated.

3. Bake the crust for 15 minutes, or until light golden in color.

TO MAKE THE FILLING

1. In a medium saucepan over medium heat, combine the brown sugar, butter, honey, heavy cream, and vanilla. Cook, stirring, for about 1 minute until the mixture dissolves well. Stir in the chopped pecans and turn off the heat.

2. Pour the pecan filling over the prebaked crust and spread it evenly using a spatula.

3. Bake the pecan pie bars for 20 minutes, or until the filling has set. The center may jiggle slightly, but it should not be liquid. Let the bars cool completely before you lift the bars out with the help of the parchment. Cut into 16 bars and serve.

➤ **Beyond the basics:** Sprinkle 1 cup of your favorite chocolate chips over the filling just before baking to add extra decadence to your pecan bars.

Fruit and Nut Bars

These granola bars are chunky, crunchy, and super filling. The base recipe can be customized with endless ingredient variations to make something different every single time.

Makes 16 bars

Prep time: 10 minutes | Cook time: 3 minutes | Bake time: 20 minutes

½ cup **honey**

¼ cup **almond butter**

1 tablespoon **unsalted butter**, at room temperature

1 teaspoon **vanilla extract**

1¼ cups old-fashioned **rolled oats**

½ cup crispy **rice cereal**

½ teaspoon ground **cinnamon**

Pinch **salt**

½ cup mixed **dried fruit**

½ cup mixed **nuts** and **seeds**

1. Place an oven rack in the middle position and preheat the oven to 350°F. Line an 8-inch square baking pan with parchment paper, leaving a few inches overhanging on two opposite sides of the pan.

2. In a small saucepan over medium heat, stir together the honey, almond butter, butter, and vanilla extract. Cook while stirring for 2 to 3 minutes, or until the mixture is melted and smooth. Remove from the heat and let cool for 5 minutes.

3. In a large bowl, combine the oats, cereal, cinnamon, and salt. Stir in the dried fruit and nuts and seeds.

4. Pour the warm honey mixture over the oat mixture and use a spatula to mix everything well. Then use the spatula to scrape the mixture into the prepared pan, pressing it firmly with your hands into an even layer.

5. Bake for 18 to 20 minutes until the granola looks slightly golden. Let the bars cool for 30 minutes in the pan. Lift the parchment paper to remove the entire block of bars. Use a serrated knife to cut it into 16 individual bars.

➤ **Swap it:** For a coconut flavor, use coconut oil instead of the butter and add ½ cup of coconut shreds or coconut flakes. The rice cereal can be swapped for any type of puffed cereal you prefer. And the almond butter can be swapped for peanut butter.

Summer Blueberry Crumble Bars

These bars have it all—they're buttery, sweet, crumbly, and loaded with fresh blueberries. There's even a touch of lemon zest in both the crust and the filling for a refreshing summer taste.

Makes 16 bars
Prep time: 15 minutes | Bake time: 50 minutes

FOR THE CRUST AND CRUMBLE

1¼ cups **quick-cooking oats**

1 cup **all-purpose flour**

1 cup packed **light brown sugar**

¾ cup cold **unsalted butter**, cut into cubes

½ teaspoon **double-acting baking powder**

1 tablespoon grated **lemon zest**

FOR THE BLUEBERRY FILLING

1¾ cups **blueberries**

2 tablespoons **light brown sugar**

1 tablespoon **all-purpose flour**

1 teaspoon **vanilla extract**

1 tablespoon grated **lemon zest**

¼ cup **blueberry jam**

TO MAKE THE CRUST AND CRUMBLE

1. Place an oven rack in the middle position and preheat the oven to 350°F. Line the bottom of an 8-inch square baking pan with parchment paper.

2. In the food processor, combine the oats, flour, brown sugar, cold butter, baking powder, and lemon zest. Pulse the ingredients until the dough looks crumbly but holds its shape when you clump it in your palm. If the dough doesn't hold together when you clump it in your hand, add 1 tablespoon of water and pulse to combine. (Alternatively, in a large bowl, whisk the oats, flour, brown sugar, baking powder, and lemon zest until combined. Add the cold butter and, using a fork, mash the butter into the flour mixture until it resembles crumbles. If the dough doesn't hold together when you clump it in your hand, add 1 tablespoon of water and mix it in with a fork to combine.)

3. Firmly press half of the crust mixture into the bottom of the prepared baking dish with your hands. Set aside the other half of the crust mixture.

4. Bake the crust for 10 minutes, or until slightly golden.

TO MAKE THE BLUEBERRY FILLING

1. In another large bowl, toss together the blueberries, brown sugar, flour, vanilla, and lemon zest. Spoon the berries over the crust in an even layer.

2. Use a spoon to dot the jam over the berries; it won't cover the entire surface.

3. Crumble the remaining half of the crust mixture over the berries.

4. Bake the bars for 35 to 40 minutes until the crumble is golden brown. Cool the bars completely and cut them into 16 squares.

➤ **Swap it:** The crust can be made entirely with oats for an oat-y, nutty flavor and a healthier twist. Just use 2 1/4 cups of oats and omit the flour. You can also use orange zest in the filling instead of lemon zest if you prefer an orange-blueberry flavor combination. Any type of berry will work here, but if you use strawberries, cut them into raspberry-size pieces and add an extra tablespoon of flour to the filling.

Perfect Lemon Bars

This two-layered dessert involves a buttery crust and a refreshing lemon top layer. These lemon bars are foolproof and can be easily adjusted to your taste.

Makes 16 bars
Prep time: 15 Minutes | Bake time: 45 Minutes

FOR THE CRUST

¾ cup **all-purpose flour**

½ cup **confectioners' sugar**

2 tablespoons **cornstarch**

Pinch **salt**

½ cup **unsalted butter**, at room temperature

FOR THE FILLING

3 tablespoons **all-purpose flour**

1 cup **granulated sugar**

3 large **eggs**

2 tablespoons grated **lemon zest**

⅓ cup freshly squeezed **lemon juice**

1 tablespoon **unsalted butter**, at room temperature

¼ cup **heavy (whipping) cream**

¼ cup **confectioners' sugar**

➤ Swap it: Make lime bars or orange bars by using the same amounts of zest and juice, but from limes or oranges instead. Or, even better, make mixed citrus bars.

TO MAKE THE CRUST

1. Place an oven rack in the middle position and preheat the oven to 375°F. Line the bottom of an 8-inch square pan with parchment paper.

2. In a large bowl, stir together the flour, confectioners' sugar, cornstarch, and salt. Add the butter. Use a fork to mash the butter into the flour mixture. It will clump at first, but keep mixing until the butter has blended in and the mixture looks like crumbs.

3. Pour the crumbs into the prepared baking pan and press them down into the bottom using your hands to form a crust. Don't press the crust against the sides of the pan.

4. Bake for 15 to 20 minutes until the crust hardens slightly.

TO MAKE THE FILLING

1. While the crust is baking, in a large bowl, whisk the flour, granulated sugar, and eggs until combined.

2. While whisking, add the lemon zest, lemon juice, butter, and heavy cream to blend.

3. Pour the filling over the prebaked crust and spread it evenly with a spatula.

4. Bake the bars for 25 minutes until the filling is set and slightly puffed. Remove and let cool for 30 minutes.

5. Cut the lemon bars into 16 (2-inch) squares. Dust with confectioners' sugar, and serve!

Divine Raspberry Cheesecake Bars

These raspberry cheesecake bars are luscious and silky smooth with their cookie crust and filling. Serve them topped with fresh berries or caramel sauce—or whatever your heart desires!

Makes 16 bars

Prep time: 20 minutes | Bake time: 1 hour 10 minutes | Chill time: 7 hours

FOR THE CRUST

1 cup **graham cracker** crumbs (about 8 whole crackers)

4 tablespoons **unsalted butter**, melted

¼ cup packed **dark brown sugar**

Pinch **salt**

FOR THE CHEESECAKE FILLING

2 (8-ounce) packages **cream cheese**, at room temperature

1 cup **granulated sugar**

¼ cup **sour cream**

2 tablespoons **all-purpose flour**

1 tablespoon **vanilla extract**

Pinch **salt**

3 large **eggs**

Fresh **raspberries**, for topping

TO MAKE THE CRUST

1. Place an oven rack in the middle position and preheat the oven to 375°F. Line the bottom of an 8-inch square baking dish with parchment paper.

2. In a medium bowl, combine the graham cracker crumbs, melted butter, brown sugar, and salt. Using a spatula, mix well to combine. With your hands, firmly press the crumbs into the bottom of the prepared baking dish and about ½ inch up the sides. It doesn't have to be perfect.

3. Bake the crust for 10 minutes. Remove from the oven and let cool.

4. Reduce the oven temperature to 325°F.

TO MAKE THE CHEESECAKE FILLING

1. In a large bowl, place the cream cheese and granulated sugar. Using a handheld electric mixer, beat the ingredients for about 2 minutes, or until fluffy, starting on the lowest speed and gradually increasing to the highest speed. Add the sour cream, flour, vanilla, and salt and mix until blended.

2. Add the eggs one at a time, mixing well on low speed after each addition. (Using low speed ensures minimal air is incorporated into the batter.)

CONTINUED

Divine Raspberry Cheesecake Bars CONTINUED

3. Pour the cheesecake topping over the cooled crust.

4. Bake for 1 hour until the filling has set but the center is slightly jiggly when you shake the pan. Cool the cheesecake in the pan at room temperature for about 1 hour, then refrigerate until set, 4 to 6 hours more.

5. Remove the pan from the refrigerator and carefully lift the cheesecake bars out of the pan using the parchment paper to help. Cut the cheesecake into 16 squares and serve topped with the raspberries.

➤ **Make it easier:** If you don't have a food processor to turn the crackers quickly into crumbs, place the graham crackers in a large resealable plastic bag. Seal the bag well. Using a rolling pin or other heavy object, gently crush the crackers into crumbs by rolling it back and forth over the plastic bag.

Pumpkin Chocolate Bars

These Pumpkin Chocolate Bars are a delicious cross between a pumpkin cookie and a chocolate chip cookie in the form of a bar.

Makes 16 bars
Prep time: 10 minutes | Bake time: 30 minutes

1⅓ cups **all-purpose flour**

¾ teaspoon **baking soda**

½ teaspoon **pumpkin pie spice** (or ground cinnamon)

Pinch **salt**

½ cup **unsalted butter**, at room temperature

¾ cup **granulated sugar**

1 large **egg**

1 teaspoon **vanilla extract**

⅔ cup canned **pumpkin purée**

1 cup **chocolate chunks**

1. Place an oven rack in the middle position and pre-heat the oven to 350°F. Line the bottom of an 8-inch baking pan with parchment paper.

2. In a medium bowl, whisk the flour, baking soda, pumpkin pie spice, and salt until combined.

3. In a large bowl, using a handheld electric mixer, cream the butter and sugar, starting on the lowest speed and gradually increasing to the highest speed, until smooth. Add the egg and vanilla and mix until combined. Add the pumpkin and mix well—don't worry if the mixture looks curdled.

4. Add the dry ingredients to the wet ingredients. Mix on low speed until combined. Use a spatula to fold in the chocolate chunks. Spread the batter evenly in the prepared pan.

5. Bake the bars for 30 minutes, or until the bars have pulled away from the sides of the pan. Cool the bars completely in the pan and cut into squares.

➤ **Beyond the basics:** This bar is crustless and has a cookie-like texture. If you want a softer, brownie-like texture, add 1 teaspoon of double-acting baking powder to the dry ingredients and 1 more egg to the recipe.

CHAPTER FOUR

Cookies

There's nothing like homemade cookies. To me, baking cookies makes your house smell like home. There's something so comforting about home-baked cookies, and they're the next easiest way to start baking (after bars, which require no shaping). Once you master the basic recipes here, try the variations for fun!

Keys to Baking Cookies

- Making cookies is a straightforward process. Most recipes begin with creaming the butter and sugar(s). The butter, in most of my recipes, has to be at room temperature so it's easier to work with. Even if the butter is melted, you'll notice the creaming of butter and sugar is usually still a part of the recipe. This step ensures the cookies puff in the oven and have an airy texture.

- The best way to divide cookie dough is with an ice cream scoop, which creates cookies of even size so they bake evenly. Scoops come in many different sizes so you can make cookies as small or big as you like. Cookies spread during baking, so space them about 1 inch apart on your prepared baking sheet.

GLAZED SUGAR COOKIES (PAGE 67)

- If you prefer a soft, cakey cookie, which spreads very little while baking, chill the cookie dough for at least 30 minutes before baking it. You can chill the formed cookies on the baking sheet or chill the dough as is, before scooping.

- Some cookies are rolled rather than scooped. As a rule of thumb, when rolling any dough, place it on a lightly floured surface. Use your hands to pat the dough roughly into the shape you want. Lightly flour your rolling pin and use it to start pushing the dough while rolling back and forth with even pressure. Rotate your dough every few seconds and continue rolling, making sure the thickness is as even as possible.

- The most important tip when rolling any dough is to check that the dough isn't sticking to your work surface. If the dough feels sticky, lightly dust the work surface, the top of the dough, or the rolling pin, if needed. That's why rotating the dough between rolling is crucial.

- Sometimes you need more than one baking sheet. When baking multiple sheets of cookies at the same time, it is ideal if both fit on the same oven rack. Two-thirds of the way through the baking time, rotate the baking sheets, front to back, to ensure even baking.

- If your oven can't handle both sheets on the same rack, use two racks: the middle rack and the upper middle rack, placing one baking sheet on each rack. Two-thirds of the way through the baking time, switch the baking sheets from the bottom rack to the top rack, and rotate them from front to back to ensure even cooking.

- Cookies can be flavored endlessly, so be as creative as you want. Enjoy the process and the aroma of cookies baking in your oven.

Checking for Doneness

Cookies have a straightforward trick to achieving chewy, soft cookie perfection: When the cookies spread and the edges start to set, but the centers still feel soft and raw, they're ready. If you prefer a crunchier cookie, wait until the centers have set, too.

You'll need to let cookies cool on the baking sheet for at least 5 minutes before transferring them to a wire rack to cool completely. This step is crucial, as the cookies need time for their centers to set outside of the oven to achieve their optimal chewy texture. Don't rush to pick them up as they can break apart.

Storage Guidelines

Once completely cooled, cookies can be stored in an airtight container at room temperature for up to 5 days. To freeze cookies, wrap your completely cooled cookies in plastic wrap, place them in an airtight container, and freeze them for up to 3 months.

To thaw the cookies, place them on the counter at room temperature overnight or for 8 to 12 hours. To warm the cookies, place the thawed cookies in a 350°F oven for 2 minutes.

You may prepare the cookie dough ahead and refrigerate it for up to 3 days before scooping and baking as directed.

To freeze unbaked cookie dough, scoop the cookies onto a parchment paper–lined baking sheet and freeze them on the baking sheet. Once frozen, place the cookie balls in a freezer-safe resealable bag and keep frozen for up to 3 months. You can bake them one at a time, as needed, from frozen, on a parchment-lined baking sheet at 350°F, adding an extra 2 minutes to the baking time noted in the recipe.

Ultimate Chocolate Chip Cookies

Everyone has their own version of the best chocolate chip cookies! Mine is on the puffy side—chewy in the center and firm on the edges. These are not too dense, are studded with chocolate, and have a strong buttery flavor.

Makes 12 cookies

Prep time: 15 minutes | Bake time: 10 minutes

½ cup **unsalted butter**, melted

½ cup **granulated sugar**

¼ cup packed **light brown sugar**

1 large **egg**, at room temperature

1 teaspoon **vanilla extract**

1½ cups **all-purpose flour**

½ teaspoon **baking soda**

⅛ teaspoon **salt**

1 cup **chocolate chips**

1. Place an oven rack in the middle position and preheat the oven to 350°F. Line a baking sheet with parchment paper.

2. In a large bowl, using a handheld electric mixer, cream the melted butter, granulated sugar, and brown sugar for about 2 minutes, or until fluffy, starting on the lowest speed and gradually increasing to the highest speed.

3. Add the egg and vanilla. Beat for another minute until smooth.

4. In a medium bowl, whisk the flour, baking soda, and salt until blended. Add the flour mixture to the butter and egg mixture and beat until the dough just comes together and looks like crumbles. It will not be smooth dough.

5. Use a spatula to fold in the chocolate chips and then use your clean hands to gather the dough into one piece. Using a 1½-inch ice cream scoop, scoop out individual cookies and place them 1 inch apart on the prepared baking sheet. Do not flatten the cookies! They will spread slightly as they bake.

CONTINUED

Ultimate Chocolate Chip Cookies

6. Bake the cookies for 10 minutes until the edges have set and the cookies have spread, but the centers are still soft. The cookies will be rather pale; don't wait for them to brown. Cool the cookies on the baking sheet for 10 minutes before transferring them to a wire rack to cool completely.

➤ **Swap it:** Add 1/2 cup of chopped nuts, pretzels, candy, or anything you like along with the chocolate chips. It's a versatile recipe!

Best Oatmeal Raisin Cookies

These cookies don't spread much in the oven and are very oat-y thanks to the minimal amount of flour.

Makes 12 cookies
Prep time: 15 minutes | Bake time: 14 minutes

6 tablespoons **unsalted butter**, at room temperature

¾ cup packed **light brown sugar**

1 large **egg**

1 teaspoon ground **cinnamon**

1 teaspoon **vanilla extract**

1⅓ cups old-fashioned **rolled oats**

¾ cup **raisins**

⅓ cup chopped **pecans**

⅓ cup **all-purpose flour**

¼ teaspoon **double-acting baking powder**

¼ teaspoon **baking soda**

Pinch **salt**

1. Place an oven rack in the middle position and preheat the oven to 350°F. Line a baking sheet with parchment paper.

2. In a large bowl, using a handheld electric mixer, cream the butter and brown sugar for 1 to 2 minutes, or until fluffy, starting on the lowest speed and gradually increasing to the highest speed. Add the egg, cinnamon, and vanilla and beat for 30 seconds more until smooth.

3. In a medium bowl, whisk the oats, raisins, pecans, flour, baking powder, baking soda, and salt until combined. Use a spatula to fold the oat mixture into the egg mixture. The dough will be a little crumbly.

4. Using a tablespoon measure, pick up golf ball–size portions of dough and place them on the cookie sheet about ½ inch apart.

5. Bake the cookies for 12 to 14 minutes, depending on their size. Remove them when the edges have set, but the centers are still soft (for a chewy cookie) or bake for 2 minutes more until the centers are set (for a crunchier cookie). Let cool on the baking sheet for 5 minutes before attempting to remove them.

➤ **Pro tip:** Make sure your butter is at room temperature—not too cold or too warm—to get the perfect oatmeal cookie. The cookie dough should not be runny when you shape your cookies. If the dough is not holding its shape before baking, add an additional 1/4 cup of oats to the dough and try again.

Decadent Brownie Cookies

A cross between chocolate cookies and fudge brownies, these delights are slightly cakey and crackly on the outside, super soft on the inside, and absolutely easy to make!

Makes 10 cookies
Prep time: 15 minutes | Bake time: 12 minutes

3 tablespoons **unsalted butter**, at room temperature

⅔ cup **semisweet chocolate** chunks, divided

¼ cup **cocoa powder**

¼ cup **all-purpose flour**

⅛ teaspoon **double-acting baking powder**

Pinch **salt**

1 large **egg**

⅓ cup **sugar**

1 teaspoon **vanilla extract**

2 tablespoons dried **cranberries**

2 tablespoons roughly chopped **hazelnuts**

1. Place an oven rack in the middle position and preheat the oven to 375°F. Line a baking sheet with parchment paper.

2. In a medium microwave-safe bowl, combine the butter and ⅓ cup of chocolate chunks. Microwave for 30 seconds. Whisk until melted and smooth. If the mixture is not smooth yet, microwave again for 15 seconds and whisk until smooth. Whisk in the cocoa powder.

3. In a small bowl, stir together the flour, baking powder, and salt. Add the flour mixture to the melted butter and cocoa powder mixture. Use a spatula to mix them together.

4. In a large bowl, combine the egg, sugar, and vanilla. Using a handheld electric mixer, whip the ingredients for at least 3 minutes, starting on the lowest speed and gradually increasing to the highest speed, until the mixture is pale yellow and nearly tripled in volume.

5. Add the chocolate mixture to the egg mixture and use a spatula to gently combine, being careful not to deflate the egg mixture too much. The cookie dough will be slightly soft and sticky.

6. Use the spatula to fold in the remaining ⅓ cup of chocolate chunks, the cranberries, and the nuts. Using a tablespoon measure, scoop out tablespoon-size portions of cookie dough and place them 1 inch apart on the prepared baking sheet. The cookies will spread.

7. Bake the cookies for 10 to 12 minutes (depending on the size of your cookie) until the edges are set. Check for doneness: The cookies will be puffed with a crackly top and slight spread. The edges will be firm to the touch, yet the cookie centers will feel soft and almost raw. Cool the cookies on the baking sheet for 5 minutes before transferring them to a wire rack to cool completely.

➤ **Pro tip:** If you need to microwave the butter and chocolate beyond the initial 30 seconds, remember to use 15-second increments to avoid burning the chocolate.

Bite-Size Coconut Macaroons

These macaroons are tiny bites of airy delight: crispy on the outside, soft on the inside, and intensely coconut-y in flavor. You'll wonder how five simple ingredients could taste so good!

Makes 20 cookies
Prep time: 10 minutes | Bake time: 25 minutes

5 cups sweetened
  flaked coconut

¾ cup **sweetened
  condensed milk**

1 teaspoon **vanilla extract**

Pinch **salt**

2 large **egg whites**

1. Place an oven rack in the middle position and preheat the oven to 325°F. Line 2 baking sheets with parchment paper.

2. In a large bowl, combine the coconut, sweetened condensed milk, and vanilla. Use a spatula to mix the ingredients well.

3. In a medium bowl, combine the egg whites and salt. Using a handheld electric mixer, whip the egg whites for about 3 minutes on the highest speed until fluffy. Lift the egg whites on the beaters: If the egg whites form stiff peaks when lifted, they are ready. If they are still too soft, whip the egg whites for 1 minute more. Using a spatula, transfer the egg whites to the coconut mixture and fold them into the batter.

4. Using a 1-inch ice cream scoop, create individual coconut balls and place them about ⅛ inch apart on the prepared baking sheets—they don't spread in the oven.

CONTINUED

Bite-Size Coconut Macaroons continued

5. Bake the macaroons for 22 to 25 minutes, switching the baking sheets two-thirds of the way through the baking time, until they're firm to the touch and slightly golden on top. Cool the macaroons on the baking sheets for 5 minutes. Carefully transfer them to a wire rack to cool completely.

➤ **Beyond the basics:** Using sweetened condensed milk is better than regular sugar and milk here in order to achieve the soft inside of the macaroon. And using sweetened coconut flakes avoids the addition of granulated sugar, which doesn't dissolve well and can create a gritty texture.

Classic Shortbread Cookies

These are ultra-buttery, crumbly cookies shaped like sticks or fingers with tiny holes in their surface. They're done when they turn golden in color.

Makes 20 cookies
Prep time: 15 minutes | Chill time: 10 minutes | Bake time: 30 minutes

1⅔ cups **all-purpose flour**
¼ cup **cornstarch**
¾ cup **confectioners' sugar**
1 cup **unsalted butter**, at room temperature
1 teaspoon **vanilla extract**
Pinch **salt**

➤ **Beyond the basics:** Piercing the cookies is done for two reasons: One is decoration—this is how a classic shortbread cookie looks. Two, piercing allows the cookies to bake evenly without air bubbles.

1. Place an oven rack in the middle position and preheat the oven to 325°F. Line an 8-inch square pan with parchment paper, letting it overhang on two opposite sides of the pan.

2. Using a fine-mesh sieve, sift the flour and cornstarch into a medium bowl. Whisk lightly to combine.

3. Using a fine-mesh sieve, sift the confectioners' sugar into a large bowl. Add the butter, vanilla, and salt. Use a handheld electric mixer to cream this mixture for about 4 minutes, gradually increasing to the highest speed.

4. Add the flour mixture to the butter mixture and beat on the lowest speed until the dough starts to come together. Using clean hands, gather the dough and firmly press into the bottom of the prepared pan, as evenly as you can. Refrigerate for 10 minutes.

5. Cut the dough lengthwise in half. Then cut each half into 10 long finger cookies. Use a fork to pierce the cookies in a decorative way.

6. Bake the cookies in the pan for 20 to 30 minutes until golden. Let cool for 10 minutes before lifting them out of the pan, using the parchment to help. Cut the cookies along their lines.

Grandma's Soft Gingersnap Cookies

Like Classic Shortbread Cookies (page 61), gingersnaps are a timeless cookie, with a distinctive molasses and ginger taste. My version is crackly topped, but soft and chewy, and pairs well with any hot drink. You can spice up the cookies as much or as little as you like.

Makes 40 cookies
Prep time: 15 minutes | Bake time: 12 minutes

1 cup **granulated sugar**

2¼ cups **all-purpose flour**

2 teaspoons **baking soda**

1 teaspoon ground **ginger**

1 teaspoon ground **cinnamon**

½ teaspoon ground **cloves**

Pinch **salt**

¾ cup **unsalted butter**, at room temperature

1 cup packed **light brown sugar**

1 large **egg**

¼ cup **molasses**

1. Place an oven rack in the middle position and preheat the oven to 375°F. Line 2 baking sheets with parchment paper.

2. Place the granulated sugar in a small bowl.

3. In a medium bowl, whisk the flour, baking soda, ginger, cinnamon, cloves, and salt until blended.

4. In a large bowl, place the butter and brown sugar. Using a handheld electric mixer, cream the butter and brown sugar for 3 minutes, or until fluffy, starting on the lowest speed and gradually increasing to the highest speed. Add the egg and molasses. Beat the mixture for 1 minute more until well blended.

5. Add the flour mixture to the butter mixture. Mix on low speed until the dough comes together. Use a 1-inch ice cream scoop to form individual cookies and roll each one into a ball with your hands. Roll the ball in the granulated sugar and place it on the prepared baking sheet. Repeat with the remaining dough, placing the cookies about 1 inch apart.

6. Bake the cookies for 10 to 12 minutes, switching the baking sheets two-thirds of the way through the baking time, until puffy and crackly on top with firm edges. Let cool on the baking sheet for 5 minutes, before transferring the cookies to a wire rack to cool completely.

➤ **Beyond the basics:** These cookies are soft, chewy, and slightly puffy; if you prefer a crispy gingerbread type of cookie, leave out the baking soda.

Easy Linzer Cookies

Linzer cookies are a classic Austrian delight that made its way to North America and, eventually, became a staple holiday treat. When I lived in Vienna, I tasted so many different variations of these buttery jam-stuffed sandwich cookies. Use this basic recipe to become familiar with the cookie, then explore the different variations and pick your favorite!

Makes 12 cookies
Prep time: 30 minutes | Bake time: 13 minutes

1¼ cups whole **hazelnuts** (or 1½ cups packed hazelnut flour)

1 cup **all-purpose flour**, plus more for the work surface

¼ teaspoon ground **cinnamon**

Pinch **salt**

4 tablespoons **unsalted butter**, at room temperature

¼ cup **granulated sugar**

1 large **egg**

1 teaspoon **vanilla extract**

2 tablespoons **confectioners' sugar**

¼ cup **raspberry jam**

1. Place an oven rack in the middle position and preheat the oven to 375°F. Line 2 baking sheets with parchment paper.

2. If using whole nuts, in your food processor, process the nuts for about 1 minute, alternating between processing and pulsing, until you have a gritty flour texture, about the size of bread crumbs. Transfer the ground nuts (or the store-bought hazelnut flour) to a medium bowl. Whisk in the all-purpose flour, cinnamon, and salt.

3. In a large bowl, using a handheld electric mixer, cream the butter and granulated sugar for about 2 minutes, until light and fluffy, starting on the lowest speed and gradually increasing to the highest speed. Use a spatula to scrape the bowl and stir the mixture to make sure it is well blended. Add the egg and vanilla to the butter mixture and beat for 1 minute more.

4. Slowly add the flour mixture and reduce the mixer speed to low until the dough forms.

CONTINUED

5. Lightly dust a work surface with flour and place the dough on it. Using a rolling pin, roll out the dough to ¼-inch thickness. Using a 2-inch heart cookie cutter, cut out 24 large hearts.

6. In the center of half the hearts, cut out small heart shapes using a ½-inch heart-shaped cookie cutter. These will be the top of the cookie sandwich. The others will be the bottom of the cookie sandwich.

7. Transfer all the cookies to the prepared baking sheets.

8. Bake the cookies for 11 to 13 minutes, switching the baking sheets two-thirds of the way through the baking time, until the edges and bottoms are golden and the tops are still a light, pale color. Let the cookies cool on the baking sheet for 5 minutes before transferring to a wire rack to cool completely.

9. Dust the top cookies (with the heart cutouts) with a thin layer of confectioners' sugar. Spread ¼ teaspoon of jam over the bottom cookies. Place a sugar-dusted top on a jam-covered bottom and press it gently to adhere. Repeat to make 12 cookie sandwiches.

➤ **Beyond the basics:** If you're grinding the nuts yourself, do not process them until they're too fine and start to release their oils (or you'll have nut butter). They need to be gritty, but tiny, in size.

Glazed Sugar Cookies

A sugar cookie is the ideal candidate for decorating. It's a sweet, yet sturdy, cookie with a good crunch, a buttery flavor, and a blank canvas to decorate however you wish. I like colored sprinkles! It's the most versatile cookie and an essential one to have in your repertoire.

Makes 20 cookies
Prep time: 15 minutes | Chill time: 30 minutes | Bake time: 12 minutes

FOR THE COOKIES

1 cup **unsalted butter**, at room temperature

⅔ cup **granulated sugar**

⅛ teaspoon **salt**

1 large **egg yolk**

2 teaspoons **vanilla extract**

2 cups **all-purpose flour**, plus more for the work surface

FOR THE GLAZE

2 cups **confectioners' sugar**

4 teaspoons light **corn syrup**

4 teaspoons **milk**

¼ teaspoon **vanilla extract**

TO MAKE THE COOKIES

1. Place an oven rack in the middle position and preheat the oven to 350°F. Line 2 baking sheets with parchment paper.

2. In a large bowl, using a handheld electric mixer, cream the butter and granulated sugar for about 2 minutes, or until fluffy, starting on the lowest speed and gradually increasing to the highest speed. Add the salt, egg yolk, and vanilla. Beat for 1 minute. Add the flour and beat until the cookie dough comes together. Refrigerate the cookie dough to chill for 30 minutes.

3. Lightly flour a work surface and place the cookie dough on it. Using a rolling pin, roll out the cookie dough to slightly less than ¼-inch thick. If the dough is sticky or seems hard to roll out, dust the surface with a little more flour. Use your cookie cutters to cut out shapes. (Don't rush when using a cookie cutter. Press the cutter down until it has cut completely through the dough.) Transfer the cookies to the prepared baking sheets. Reroll the scraps and repeat with the remaining dough.

CONTINUED

4. Bake the cookies for 10 to 12 minutes, switching the baking sheets two-thirds of the way through the cooking time, until they're golden in color. Let the cookies cool for 10 minutes before transferring them to a wire rack to cool completely.

TO MAKE THE GLAZE

1. While the cookies cool, in a small bowl, whisk the confectioners' sugar, corn syrup, milk, and vanilla until smooth. Adjust the consistency of the glaze by adding more confectioners' sugar or milk, as needed (if it's too thin, add more confectioners' sugar; if too thick, add more milk). You want a spreadable consistency; the glaze will harden as it sets.

2. Decorate the cooled cookies with the glaze, as desired.

   ➤ **Swap it:** Flavor the basic cookie dough to make these cookies your own. Add 1 teaspoon of your favorite spice (maybe cinnamon?), 1 teaspoon of an extract (I like almond), or 1 tablespoon of citrus zest.

CHAPTER FIVE

Quick Breads + Muffins

Baking a quick bread or muffins is an easy way to make something tender and delicious in no time. These recipes need only bowls, a whisk, and a rubber spatula—no electric mixer or other fancy tools required.

Keys to Baking Quick Breads + Muffins

- The secret to tender breads and muffins is a simple one: Keep the lumps in your batter! In other words, don't overmix your batter. Overmixing a muffin or quick bread batter will develop the flour proteins (similar to kneading bread dough), which results in a chewy texture (like a sandwich bread) rather than a soft, tender bite.

- Lumps are the indicator that you have not overworked your batter. They will also create pockets of tenderness throughout the quick bread and muffins.

- You'll notice quick breads and muffin recipes need two bowls—one for dry ingredients and one for wet ingredients. Each component (dry and wet) has to be mixed separately before being combined. Once you do combine them, however, minimal mixing is all

◀ ULTIMATE BANANA BREAD (PAGE 73)

that is needed. A rubber spatula is best to blend the batter together. Blend the batter until no more streaks of flour are visible, but lumps remain.

- When filling the muffin pans with batter, fill them about three-fourths full. This allows the muffins to rise to the top and form a beautiful dome.

- Each of the recipes in this chapter can be used to make either a quick bread or muffins—so, a quick bread recipe can easily be made into muffins and a muffin recipe can easily be made into a quick bread. You'll just need to adjust the baking time. In general, a muffin pan filled with batter usually needs 18 to 22 minutes to bake; a loaf pan needs 55 to 60 minutes.

- Always bake muffins and quick breads on the top middle rack of the oven.

Checking for Doneness

There are a few tips to test for doneness. The easiest way to check for doneness is the toothpick method. During baking, you'll notice muffins and quick breads rise well. Once the baking time is complete, that's when you'll do the test.

Insert a toothpick into the center of the bread or a muffin. Remove it, and if it comes out clean, or with only a few crumbs attached, it's done. But, if the toothpick has raw batter on it, it needs a few more minutes in the oven. Then you can check it again.

Another method to check doneness is by touch. When you touch a baked muffin or quick bread, it should be springy to the touch. That means if you push gently on the surface of the muffin, it should spring back.

Storage Guidelines

Completely cooled muffins and quick breads keep well in an airtight container at room temperature for up to 3 days. After that they start to dry out.

Muffins can also be wrapped well in plastic wrap and frozen to preserve their freshness. When you're ready to enjoy them, simply remove them from the freezer and thaw at room temperature overnight or for 8 to 12 hours. You can warm them in a 350°F oven for 2 minutes after thawing.

Ultimate Banana Bread

This banana bread recipe is the only one you'll ever need. It's not oily, heavy, too sweet, or too dense. Instead, it is a perfectly tender and moist yet light bread infused with banana flavor.

Makes 1 loaf
Prep time: 10 minutes | Bake time: 1 hour

2 large, very ripe **bananas**

⅔ cup packed **light brown sugar**

⅓ cup **canola oil**

⅓ cup **buttermilk**

1 large **egg**

1 teaspoon **vanilla extract**

1½ cups **all-purpose flour**

¾ teaspoon **double-acting baking powder**

¾ teaspoon **baking soda**

1 teaspoon ground **cinnamon**

Pinch **salt**

½ cup chopped **walnuts**

1. Place an oven rack in the top middle position and preheat the oven to 375°F. Line a 9-by-5-inch loaf pan with parchment paper.

2. In a large bowl, using a fork, mash the bananas until smooth. Add the brown sugar, canola oil, buttermilk, egg, and vanilla. Whisk well to combine.

3. In a medium bowl, whisk the flour, baking powder, baking soda, cinnamon, and salt until combined.

4. Use a spatula to gently mix the flour mixture into the banana mixture until you no longer see streaks of flour in the wet mixture. Fold in the walnuts, and pour the batter into the prepared loaf pan.

5. Bake the bread for 20 minutes. Lower the oven temperature to 350°F and bake for 30 to 40 minutes more, until a toothpick inserted into the middle of the loaf comes out clean. If it doesn't come out clean, bake for 10 minutes more and retest the loaf. Let the banana bread cool in the pan for 15 to 20 minutes before transferring it to a wire rack to cool completely.

➤ **Pro tip:** If your bananas aren't quite ripe enough, place them on a baking sheet and bake in a 325°F oven for 10 minutes until they turn brown.

Coffee Cake Muffins

These muffins are tender little cakes with a spike of cinnamon and vanilla and topped with a sweet, buttery, crunchy crumble.

Makes 12 muffins
Prep time: 10 minutes | Bake time: 20 minutes

FOR THE TOPPING

⅓ cup **all-purpose flour**

⅓ cup packed **light brown sugar**

½ teaspoon ground **cinnamon**

3 tablespoons **butter**, at room temperature

FOR THE MUFFINS

1½ cups **all-purpose flour**

2 teaspoons **double-acting baking powder**

½ teaspoon ground **cinnamon**

¼ teaspoon **baking soda**

Pinch **salt**

¾ cup packed **light brown sugar**

¾ cup **sour cream**

⅓ cup **canola oil**

2 large **eggs**

1 teaspoon **vanilla extract**

TO MAKE THE TOPPING

1. In a small bowl, whisk the flour, brown sugar, and cinnamon until blended.

2. Add the butter and, using a fork, mash it into the flour mixture until the topping looks like crumbles.

TO MAKE THE MUFFINS

1. Place an oven rack in the top middle position and preheat the oven to 375°F. Line a 12-cup muffin pan with muffin liners.

2. In a medium bowl, whisk the flour, baking powder, cinnamon, baking soda, and salt until blended.

3. In a large bowl, combine the brown sugar, sour cream, oil, eggs, and vanilla. Whisk until smooth. Add the dry ingredients to the wet ingredients and use a spatula to blend them together. The batter will be lumpy. Don't attempt to make it smooth. Evenly divide the batter among the prepared muffin cups, filling each liner about three-fourths full.

4. Top each muffin with about 1½ teaspoons of the crumble topping.

5. Bake for 20 minutes until the muffins puff and a toothpick inserted into the middle of a muffin comes out clean. Cool the muffins in the pan for 5 minutes. Carefully transfer them to a wire rack to cool completely.

▷ **Swap it:** Skip the cinnamon for a vanilla-flavored coffee cake. These muffins are also easily flavored with berries or nuts: Add 1 cup of fresh or frozen raspberries or blueberries (no need to thaw, if frozen) or ½ cup of chopped nuts of your choice.

Double Chocolate Mini-Muffins

These little gems pack an intense chocolate flavor and a melt-in-your-mouth texture, with bonus chocolate pieces. Their miniature size makes them an exquisite little treat. Plus, they bake in just 10 minutes, so they can deliver a quick chocolate fix when you need it!

Makes 24 mini-muffins
Prep time: 10 minutes | Bake time: 10 minutes

1¼ cups **all-purpose flour**

1¼ teaspoons **double-acting baking powder**

¼ teaspoon **baking soda**

Pinch **salt**

¾ cup **sugar**

⅓ cup **cocoa powder**

1 large **egg**

¾ cup **sour cream**

¼ cup **canola oil**

1 teaspoon **vanilla extract**

1½ cups finely chopped **chocolate**

1. Place an oven rack in the top middle position and preheat the oven to 375°F. Line a 24-cup mini-muffin pan with 24 mini-muffin liners.

2. In a medium bowl, whisk the flour, baking powder, baking soda, and salt until combined.

3. In a large bowl, whisk the sugar, cocoa powder, egg, sour cream, canola oil, and vanilla until smooth. Add the dry ingredients to the wet ingredients and, using a spatula, mix them to combine. Fold in the chocolate pieces. Evenly divide the batter among the prepared mini-muffin cups, filling each liner about three-fourths full.

4. Bake the muffins for 8 to 10 minutes until a toothpick inserted into the center of a muffin comes out clean. Cool the muffins in the pan for 5 minutes. Carefully transfer them to a wire rack to cool completely.

➢ **Beyond the basics:** Add ½ cup of finely chopped nuts for crunch. Or top each cooled muffin with a teaspoon of Nutella.

Chai Date Bread with Orange Glaze

This quick bread is flavored with a homemade chai spice blend, orange zest, and sweet dates. Thanks to the dates, it stays fresh and moist for days.

Makes 1 loaf
Prep time: 20 minutes | Bake time: 1 hour

FOR THE LOAF

1 cup minced pitted **dates**

½ cup hot **water**

1 cup **all-purpose flour**

1 teaspoon **double-acting baking powder**

1 teaspoon **baking soda**

1½ teaspoons ground **cinnamon**

1½ teaspoons ground **ginger**

⅛ teaspoon ground **cardamom**

⅛ teaspoon ground **cloves**

Pinch **salt**

Dash freshly ground **black pepper**

⅓ cup **canola oil**

½ cup packed **light brown sugar**

1 large **egg**

1 tablespoon grated **orange zest**

TO MAKE THE LOAF

1. Place an oven rack in the top middle position and preheat the oven to 375°F. Line a 9-by-5-inch loaf pan with parchment paper.

2. In a medium bowl, combine the dates and hot water.

3. In another medium bowl, whisk the flour, baking powder, baking soda, cinnamon, ginger, cardamom, cloves, salt, and pepper until blended.

4. In a large bowl, combine the oil, brown sugar, egg, water-date mixture, and orange zest. Whisk to combine.

5. Use a spatula to mix the dry ingredients into the wet ingredients, folding the batter together until just blended and no more streaks of flour appear. Pour the batter into the prepared loaf pan.

6. Bake the bread for about 1 hour, then check for doneness. Insert a toothpick into the center of the loaf. If it comes out clean, with only very fine crumbs attached, it is done. If not, bake for a few minutes more and test again. Remove and let cool for 10 minutes. Remove the slightly cooled loaf from the pan and place it on a wire rack to cool completely.

FOR THE GLAZE

¼ cup **cream cheese**, at room temperature

½ cup **confectioners' sugar**

2 tablespoons **milk**

1 teaspoon **vanilla extract**

1 teaspoon grated **orange zest**

TO MAKE THE GLAZE

1. While the loaf bakes, in a small bowl, combine the cream cheese, confectioners' sugar, milk, vanilla, and orange zest. Whisk until smooth. The glaze can be as runny or thick as you like. Add more milk for a thinner glaze or more confectioners' sugar for a thicker glaze.

2. Pour the glaze over the completely cooled loaf.

➤ **Swap it:** Turn this recipe into muffins, if you prefer. Just adjust the baking time to 15 to 18 minutes.

Studded Blueberry Muffins

There's nothing like a good blueberry muffin! I love a tender, buttery muffin bursting with blueberries. You can make these with fresh or frozen blueberries.

Makes 12 muffins
Prep time: 15 minutes | Bake time: 20 minutes

2 cups **all-purpose flour**

1 tablespoon **double-acting baking powder**

Pinch **salt**

1 cup **buttermilk**

1 cup **sugar**

⅓ cup **unsalted butter,** melted (or canola oil)

1 large **egg**

1 teaspoon **vanilla extract**

1½ cups **blueberries,** fresh or frozen

1. Place an oven rack in the top middle position and preheat the oven to 400°F. Line a 12-cup muffin pan with 12 muffin liners.

2. In a medium bowl, whisk the flour, baking powder, and salt until blended.

3. In a large bowl, whisk the buttermilk, sugar, melted butter, egg, and vanilla until combined. Add the dry ingredients to the wet ingredients and, using a spatula, mix them together well. Do not overmix the batter. Some visible lumps in the batter are okay, but no visible streaks of flour should remain.

4. Use a spatula to gently fold in the blueberries without bruising or crushing them. (There's no need to thaw the berries if you're using frozen.) Spoon the batter into the prepared muffin pan, filling each liner about three-fourths full.

5. Bake the muffins for 20 minutes until a toothpick inserted into the center of a muffin comes out clean. Let the muffins cool for 10 minutes in the pan before removing.

➤ **Swap it:** Substitute chocolate chips for the blueberries for a decadent breakfast treat!

Tender Whole-Wheat Apple Muffins

These muffins are hearty, tender, and perfectly balanced. They're packed with apples and spiced with cinnamon. The whole-wheat flour adds extra fiber and a nutty taste.

Makes 12 muffins
Prep time: 15 minutes | Rest time: 10 minutes | Bake time: 18 minutes

1½ cups **whole-wheat flour**

1 teaspoon **baking soda**

Pinch **salt**

1 large **egg**

¾ cup **buttermilk** (or plain yogurt)

⅔ cup packed **light brown sugar**

¼ cup **canola oil**

1 teaspoon ground **cinnamon**

2 **apples**, peeled, cored, and grated

1. Place an oven rack in the top middle position and preheat the oven to 375°F. Line a 12-cup muffin pan with 12 muffin liners.

2. In a medium bowl, whisk the flour, baking soda, and salt until blended.

3. In a large bowl, combine the egg, buttermilk, brown sugar, canola oil, and cinnamon. Whisk well to combine. Add the flour mixture and the apples. Use a spatula to mix everything until blended. Do not overmix the batter; it should still have some visible lumps. Evenly divide the batter among the prepared muffin cups, filling each liner about three-fourths full. Let the muffins rest for 10 minutes so the whole-wheat flour absorbs some moisture.

4. Bake the muffins for 15 to 18 minutes until a toothpick inserted into the center of a muffin comes out clean. Cool the muffins in the pan for 5 minutes. Carefully transfer them to a wire rack to cool completely.

➤ **Make it easier:** Leave the apples unpeeled. The peel does not affect the recipe outcome, and you might decide that you like the muffins with bits of peel even better than without.

Basic Biscuits

This basic biscuit recipe calls for you to pay special attention to the temperature of the ingredients: For extremely flaky biscuits, make sure the biscuits are COLD and your oven is HOT at the time of baking.

Makes 16 biscuits
Prep time: 20 minutes | Bake time: 15 minutes

1¾ cups **all-purpose flour**, plus more for the work surface

1 tablespoon **double-acting baking powder**

1 teaspoon **sugar**

½ teaspoon **baking soda**

¼ teaspoon **salt**

6 tablespoons **unsalted butter,** frozen

¾ cup cold **buttermilk**

➤ **Pro tip:** If you've taken a long time to make your biscuits and the dough has warmed up, refrigerate the biscuits until the dough is cold again before popping them into the hot oven.

1. Place an oven rack in the top middle position and preheat the oven to 450°F. Line a baking sheet with parchment paper.

2. In a large bowl, whisk the flour, baking powder, sugar, baking soda, and salt until combined.

3. Using a box grater, grate the frozen butter into the flour mixture. Using a fork, toss the flour and butter until the flour evenly coats the butter. Add the buttermilk and swirl it around with the fork until dough forms.

4. Lightly flour a work surface and turn the dough out onto it. Using your clean hands, pat it down and form it into a rectangle about 4 inches by 6 inches.

5. With a rolling pin, roll the dough into a rectangle about ½-inch thick. Use a 2-inch round cookie cutter to cut out circles, or cut the dough into 2-inch squares with a knife. Place the biscuits on the prepared baking sheet.

6. Bake the biscuits for 8 minutes. Reduce the oven temperature to 375°F and bake for 4 to 7 minutes more, until they are puffed and slightly golden on the bottom. Transfer to a wire rack to cool.

Savory Cheese Muffins

Imagine your favorite cheeses, herbs, and spices baked into a tender pillowy muffin. These savory treats are made the same way you make a sweet muffin, only flavored differently. These muffins pair very well with a soup or salad!

Makes 12 muffins
Prep time: 15 minutes | Bake time: 30 minutes

2 cups **all-purpose flour**

2 teaspoons **double-acting baking powder**

2 teaspoons **sugar**

½ teaspoon **baking soda**

½ teaspoon freshly ground **black pepper**

¼ teaspoon **salt**

1 cup grated **cheddar cheese**

½ cup fresh **herb leaves** (such as parsley, oregano, or thyme)

1½ cups **buttermilk** (or plain yogurt)

¼ cup light **olive oil**

1 large **egg**

1. Place an oven rack in the top middle position and preheat the oven to 375°F. Line a 12-cup muffin pan with muffin liners and coat them with cooking spray. The cooking spray is important because the cheese tends to stick to the liners.

2. In a large bowl, whisk the flour, baking powder, sugar, baking soda, pepper, and salt until combined. Add the cheddar cheese and herbs. Toss the ingredients well to combine. The flour needs to coat the cheese and herbs very well.

3. In another large bowl, whisk the buttermilk, olive oil, and egg until smooth.

4. Add the dry ingredients to the wet ingredients and use a spatula to fold the batter together. Evenly divide the batter among the prepared muffin cups, filling each liner about three-fourths full.

5. Bake the muffins for 25 to 30 minutes, or until a toothpick inserted into the center of a muffin comes out clean. Let cool for 10 minutes before removing from the pan to cool completely.

➤ **Make it easier:** Using dried herbs instead of fresh herbs is a time-saver and a more convenient option if you don't keep fresh herbs on hand. Use 2 tablespoons of dried herbs in place of the fresh herbs in this recipe. Choose your favorite single herb, or combine a few and see what fun new flavor you can create.

CHAPTER SIX

Cakes

A cake is heartwarming, comforting, and welcoming. Cake batter begins with creaming the butter and sugar. Add the eggs and slowly incorporate the remaining ingredients. You end up with a delicious cake you can eat as is, layer and frost, dust with confectioners' sugar, or drizzle with a satiny glaze.

Keys to Baking Cake

· Cake batters have a base of butter and sugar creamed together—that's how they develop a fine, tender, buttery texture. The eggs (just yolks, just whites, or both) can then be whipped into the butter mixture.

· To line a round cake pan, cut a parchment paper round that is larger than the size of your cake pan. Fold the parchment paper in half, and again, and a third time until you end up with a triangle shape. Flip your cake pan upside down, and hold the tip of the triangle at the center of the cake pan bottom. Trim the paper to match the pan's edge. Then unfold the triangle into a perfect circle to line your cake pan.

· To make cake layers, divide the batter into two, three, or even four cake pans. That way you don't have to worry about neatly slicing one tall cake into layers.

ZESTY LEMON BUNDT CAKE (PAGE 92)

- While baking your cakes, keep the oven door closed. Each time you open the oven door during baking, the rising process is disturbed and the structure of the cake will be compromised. You can safely open the oven door and have a look at the cake two-thirds of the way through baking.

- It's best to freeze the cake layers for 30 to 45 minutes before frosting. This ensures the the cake layers are sturdy enough to hold up to frosting, filling, and stacking. Always remember to start with cold cake layers and cold frosting. When frosting is chilled it may harden a bit but, as you start to work with it, it will soften.

- Frost each layer separately. Use a spoon and dollop equal amounts of frosting over the top of each cake layer. Spread the frosting using a spatula. Then pick up each layer and stack them one at a time. If you're also adding fruit between each layer, add it on top of the frosting before you set down the next cake layer. Finally, add the top layer that you'd set aside and frost that one too.

- To frost the sides of a cake: Start with a small amount of frosting and spread it bit by bit. If you're aiming for a thick frosting layer, layer it on. Start with a thin layer. Refrigerate the frosted cake for 30 minutes and repeat the same thin layer of frosting—and so on until the frosting is thick enough for you.

- If you're rushed on time but still need to whip up a fancy cake, try either a "naked" cake or sheet pan cake. A naked cake has minimal frosting, if any, on the sides (so you can see the layers). A sheet pan cake is baked in a single layer on a large sheet pan and topped once with a simple frosting. A sprinkle of nuts or fruit gives you an impressive-looking cake in no time.

- All of my cake recipes can be made into cupcakes. Each cake recipe will make about 36 cupcakes, so you'll need 3 standard (12-cup) muffin pans. Only the baking times need to be adjusted. Most cupcakes bake for 18 to 22 minutes.

Checking for Doneness

You can determine if a cake is done by testing it with a toothpick. Insert a toothpick into the center of the cake and, if it comes out clean, the cake is done. Even if you see tiny pieces of dry cake crumbs on the toothpick, it still means the cake is cooked through. Remove the cake from the oven and let it cool in the pan for at least 15 minutes.

Storage Guidelines

Cakes are stored differently depending on which stage of preparation you've reached. Baked cake layers, unfrosted, can be wrapped individually in parchment paper, then plastic wrap, and stored at room temperature before frosting within 2 days. These same cake layers can be wrapped and refrigerated for 5 days, or frozen for up to 3 months.

A frosted cake you plan to serve within a few days can be refrigerated, well wrapped, for up to 1 week. If you're living in a cold place and your room temperature is cool, you can also store it on the counter, but for just 2 days, at most. However, if your cake contains fruit, whipped cream, or cream cheese, it must be kept refrigerated.

There are two ways to refrigerate a frosted cake: (1) Place the frosted cake on a tray or a large plate and place a large bowl over the cake to cover the cake entirely (making sure the bowl doesn't touch the cake) and refrigerate it. (2) Refrigerate the cake uncovered to chill for 1 hour until the frosting hardens and the layers are solidly stuck together. Wrap the chilled cake in plastic wrap. It's best to wrap the cake and plate together to minimize any refrigerator odors from seeping into your frosted cake.

To freeze fully frosted and layered cakes, you need to do it in stages. Start by freezing the cake layers. Then fill and layer the cakes. Do not frost the outside of the cake, just the layers. Now you can wrap it well in plastic wrap and freeze it. Once you're ready to finish it, take the cake out of the freezer and frost the outside while the cake is still frozen; the frosting adheres better to the cake this way. Alternatively, you can wrap and freeze the fully frosted cake for up to 2 months (but I don't recommend this because many frostings lose their texture when thawed). If you decide to try it, thaw the cake in the refrigerator overnight and serve it within the week.

Zesty Lemon Bundt Cake

In this recipe you'll learn how to incorporate air into eggs and see how this creates an unbeatable cottony-soft texture!

Makes 1 cake
Prep time: 20 minutes | Bake time: 30 minutes

4 tablespoons **unsalted butter**, melted, plus more for preparing the pan

3 cups **cake flour**, plus more for preparing the pan

3 teaspoons **double-acting baking powder**

½ teaspoon **salt**, divided

6 large **eggs**, separated

1½ cups **sugar**, divided

½ cup **milk**

¼ cup **canola oil**

¼ cup freshly squeezed **lemon juice**

2 tablespoons grated **lemon zest**

➤ **Beyond the basics:** When whipping egg whites, make sure your beaters and bowls are clean and completely free of any traces of fat or egg yolks. A trace of egg yolk or fat will prevent the egg whites from whipping properly.

1. Place an oven rack in the top middle position and preheat the oven to 350°F. Butter the inside of 12-cup Bundt pan. Sprinkle a spoonful of flour into the pan, tapping the flour around the pan. Shake off any excess.

2. Using a fine-mesh sieve, sift the flour, baking powder, and ¼ teaspoon salt into a large bowl.

3. In another large bowl, whip the egg whites, ¾ cup of the sugar, and remaining ¼ teaspoon salt for 3 to 4 minutes on high speed until the egg whites form stiff peaks.

4. In another large bowl, beat the egg yolks and the remaining ¾ cup of sugar for 2 minutes until foamy. Add the milk, canola oil, melted butter, lemon juice, and lemon zest. Beat for 2 minutes more, until smooth. Add the flour mixture to the egg yolk mixture and mix until smooth.

5. Use a spatula to fold the egg white mixture into the batter, being careful not to deflate the egg whites. Pour the batter into the pan.

6. Bake for 25 to 30 minutes until a toothpick inserted into the center comes out clean. Cool in the pan before transferring to a wire rack to cool completely. Enjoy the cake as it is, or top it with your favorite glaze.

Basic Yellow Cake

Also known as a good old vanilla cake, it's rich, moist, and tender, infused with vanilla and butter flavors. This cake can be eaten plain or covered with your favorite frosting.

Makes 3 cake layers
Prep time: 15 minutes | Bake time: 28 minutes

1½ cups **sugar**

½ cup **unsalted butter**, at room temperature

⅓ cup **canola oil**

3 large **eggs**

1½ cups **buttermilk**

2 teaspoons **vanilla extract**

3⅓ cups **all-purpose flour**

4 teaspoons **double-acting baking powder**

Pinch **salt**

➤ **Beyond the basics:**
If you like the idea of a confetti cake (and who doesn't?), use a rubber spatula to fold ½ cup of rainbow sprinkles into the batter once all the ingredients are blended, then sprinkle another ½ cup of rainbow sprinkles over the frosted cake.

1. Place an oven rack in the top middle position and preheat the oven to 350°F. Line 3 (9-inch) round cake pans with parchment paper.

2. In a large bowl, cream the sugar and butter for about 2 minutes, or until fluffy, starting on the lowest speed and gradually increasing to the highest speed. Add the oil and eggs and beat for 2 minutes more on high speed until the mixture turns lighter in color and becomes fluffy again. Add the buttermilk and vanilla and mix until blended.

3. In a medium bowl, whisk the flour, baking powder, and salt until no lumps remain. Add the dry ingredients to the wet ingredients and mix on very low speed until the batter looks smooth, stopping to scrape the bowl, as needed, to make sure the batter is well blended. Evenly divide the batter among the prepared cake pans.

4. Bake the cakes for 25 to 28 minutes, until a toothpick inserted into the centers comes out clean. Let the cakes cool in the pans at room temperature for 15 to 20 minutes before removing them to a wire rack to cool completely. Frost, freeze, or chill the cakes, as needed.

Flourless Chocolate Cake

This is a dense cake with an intense chocolate flavor and is often called a chocolate torte. The cake can be garnished with a simple dusting of confectioners' sugar, a fancy chocolate ganache, or bright, colorful fresh raspberries.

GAS MARK 5

Makes 1 cake

Prep time: 10 minutes | Bake time: 28 minutes

118mL ½ cup **unsalted butter**, plus more for preparing the cake pan

350mL 1½ cups **chocolate** chunks

234 mL 1 cup **sugar**

Pinch **salt**

2 teaspoons **vanilla extract**

4 large **eggs**

156 mL ⅔ cup **cocoa powder**

1. Place an oven rack in the top middle position and preheat the oven to 375°F. Lightly coat an 8-inch round cake pan with a bit of butter. Line the pan with parchment paper and coat the paper with butter.

2. In a medium microwave-safe bowl, combine the chocolate chunks and butter. Microwave on high power for 1 minute. Whisk the butter and chocolate until smooth. If the mixture doesn't become smooth, microwave for 15 seconds more and whisk again.

3. Add the sugar, salt, vanilla, and eggs, whisking until smooth. Add the cocoa powder and whisk until smooth. Pour the batter into the prepared pan.

4. Bake for 22 to 28 minutes until the cake has set and doesn't jiggle when shaken. Let the cake cool in the pan for 15 minutes before serving. Garnish as desired.

➤ **Make it easier:** You'll be tempted to microwave the bowl for 3 or 4 minutes to make sure the chocolate has fully melted. But start with just 1 minute and whisk the chocolate well after that. If it needs more time, microwave only for 15 seconds more and whisk. If you microwave it too long, the chocolate will burn.

Birthday Cake

Making this cake involves alternating the wet ingredients and dry ingredients into the butter mixture. The cake flour gives a tender crumb to this festive cake.

Makes 2 cake layers
Prep time: 15 minutes | Bake time: 35 minutes

4 large **egg whites**, at room temperature

1¼ cups **buttermilk**

2¼ cups **cake flour** (or 2 cups all-purpose flour, plus ¼ cup cornstarch)

2 teaspoons **double-acting baking powder**

Pinch **salt**

½ cup **unsalted butter**, at room temperature

1½ cups **sugar**

2 teaspoons **vanilla extract**

1. Place an oven rack in the top middle position and preheat the oven to 350°F. Line 2 (9-inch) round cake pans with parchment paper.

2. In a medium bowl, whisk the egg whites and buttermilk until well blended.

3. In another medium bowl, whisk the flour, baking powder, and salt until combined.

4. In a large bowl, beat the butter, sugar, and vanilla for 2 minutes, or until light and fluffy, starting on low and gradually increasing to the highest speed.

5. Add one-third of the dry ingredients to the butter mixture and mix on low speed for a few seconds. Add half of the wet ingredients and continue mixing on low speed. Continue alternating dry and wet ingredients until complete. Evenly divide the batter between the prepared cake pans.

6. Bake for 32 to 35 minutes, until a toothpick inserted into the centers comes out clean. Let cool in the pans for 15 minutes before transferring to a wire rack to cool completely. Frost, freeze, or chill the cakes, as needed.

➤ **Beyond the basics:** To make a buttercream frosting, whip ¾ cup of unsalted butter, at room temperature, until pale and fluffy. Add 2½ cups of confectioners' sugar, 2 teaspoons of vanilla extract, and a pinch of salt. Beat for 2 to 3 minutes more until smooth. Add 2 tablespoons of milk of choice, beat for another minute, then chill or use right away.

Ultimate Carrot Cake

This carrot cake is flavored with a bit of orange, which strikes the perfect balance with the carrot and cinnamon. Unlike most cake recipes, this carrot cake is prepared more like a muffin or quick bread.

Makes 2 cake layers
Prep time: 20 minutes | Bake time: 30 minutes

2¾ cups **all-purpose flour**

2 teaspoons **baking soda**

2 teaspoons **cinnamon**

Pinch **salt**

½ cup **unsalted butter**, melted

4 large **eggs**

¼ cup **canola oil**

1 cup packed **light brown sugar**

1 cup **granulated sugar**

⅓ cup **buttermilk**

2 tablespoons grated **orange zest**

2 tablespoons freshly squeezed **orange juice**

3 cups shredded **carrots**

1 cup shredded **coconut**

1 cup chopped **pecans** or walnuts

1. Place an oven rack in the top middle position and preheat the oven to 375°F. Line 2 (9-inch) round cake pans with parchment paper.

2. In a medium bowl, whisk the flour, baking soda, cinnamon, and salt until combined.

3. In a large bowl, combine the melted butter, eggs, canola oil, brown sugar, granulated sugar, buttermilk, orange zest, and orange juice. Whisk until smooth. Add the dry ingredients to the wet ingredients and whisk to blend them together.

4. Add the carrots, coconut, and pecans. Using a rubber spatula, fold them into the batter, making sure to evenly distribute the carrots and incorporate all the flour mixture. Evenly divide the batter between the prepared cake pans.

5. Bake for 30 minutes until a toothpick inserted into the centers comes out clean. Let cool in the pans for 20 minutes before removing them to a wire rack to cool completely. Frost, freeze, or chill the cakes, as needed.

> **Pro tip:** Make sure the carrots aren't wet when adding them to the cake batter. If they look too wet, simply squeeze the excess water from the carrots by pressing them between two kitchen towels or two paper towels.

Red Velvet Cupcakes

This chocolate cake gets its bright red color from food coloring and its tang comes from buttermilk. The cream cheese frosting brings it all together.

Makes 36 cupcakes

Prep time: 20 minutes | Bake time: 30 minutes | Chill time: 1 hour

FOR THE CUPCAKES

2 cups **all-purpose flour**

⅓ cup **cornstarch**

⅓ cup **cocoa powder**

2 teaspoons **baking soda**

1 teaspoon **double-acting baking powder**

Pinch **salt**

3 large **eggs**

2 cups **granulated sugar**

1 cup **buttermilk**

4 tablespoons **unsalted butter**, melted

¼ cup **canola oil**

1 teaspoon **vanilla extract**

½ teaspoon **white vinegar**

2 tablespoons **red food coloring**

½ cup boiling **water**

TO MAKE THE CUPCAKES

1. Place an oven rack in the top middle position and preheat the oven to 375°F. Line 3 muffin pans with cupcake liners.

2. In a large bowl, combine the flour, cornstarch, cocoa powder, baking soda, baking powder, and salt. Whisk until blended.

3. In another large bowl, beat the eggs and granulated sugar for 4 minutes, or until fluffy, starting on low and gradually increasing to the highest speed. Add the buttermilk, melted butter, canola oil, vanilla, vinegar, and food coloring. Beat until mixed. Continue mixing and gradually add the boiling water, beating until combined. Add the dry ingredients and mix on low speed until smooth and well blended. Evenly divide the batter among the prepared muffin cups.

4. Bake for 20 to 30 minutes until a toothpick inserted into the center of the cupcakes comes out clean. Let cool in the pans for 20 minutes before removing them to cool completely before frosting.

CONTINUED

Red Velvet Cupcakes CONTINUED

FOR THE FROSTING

12 ounces **cream cheese**, at room temperature

4 tablespoons **unsalted butter**, at room temperature

2 cups **confectioners' sugar**

1 teaspoon **vanilla extract**

TO MAKE THE FROSTING

1. In a medium bowl, beat the cream cheese and butter together for 4 minutes, or until light and fluffy, on high speed.

2. Add the confectioners' sugar and vanilla and beat for 2 minutes more until smooth and creamy. If the frosting is too thin, add more confectioners' sugar a little at a time.

3. Frost the tops of the cupcakes. Refrigerate to chill. Serve cold.

➤ **Beyond the basics:** Use a vegetable peeler to shave shreds from a white chocolate bar and sprinkle them over the cupcakes for a beautiful and easy finish.

Easy Black Forest Cake

Layers of rich chocolate sponge cake sandwich a sweet cherry filling and vanilla whipped cream. Every bite is a dream.

Makes 1 cake

Prep time: 20 minutes | Cook time: 5 minutes | Bake time: 30 minutes

FOR THE CHERRY FILLING

3 tablespoons cold **water**

¼ cup **cornstarch**

¼ cup **granulated sugar**

3 cups pitted **cherries**, plus more for garnish

FOR THE WHIPPED CREAM

3 cups **heavy (whipping) cream**

½ cup **confectioners' sugar**

1 teaspoon **vanilla extract**

Pinch **salt**

FOR THE CAKE

1 cup **granulated sugar**

½ cup **unsalted butter**, at room temperature

6 large **eggs**, separated

1 teaspoon **vanilla extract**

1½ cups **all-purpose flour**

⅔ cup **cocoa powder**

¼ cup **cornstarch**

1 teaspoon **double-acting baking powder**

1 teaspoon **baking soda**

Pinch **salt**

TO MAKE THE CHERRY FILLING

1. Make the cherry mixture first so it has time to cool. In a medium saucepan, whisk the cold water and cornstarch until smooth. Add the granulated sugar and whisk again. Add the cherries and stir to combine.

2. Place the pan over medium heat and cook until the filling bubbles. Cook for another 3 minutes until the mixture thickens. Remove from the heat and let cool, either on the counter or in the refrigerator. The filling can be prepared up to 2 days in advance and kept refrigerated.

TO MAKE THE WHIPPED CREAM

1. In a large bowl, combine the heavy cream, confectioners' sugar, vanilla, and salt. Using clean beaters, beat the ingredients for about 6 minutes until fluffy and stiff peaks form.

2. Refrigerate the whipped cream until needed. The whipped cream may be prepared up to 2 days in advance and kept refrigerated.

CONTINUED

Easy Black Forest Cake CONTINUED

TO MAKE THE CAKE

1. Place an oven rack in the top middle position and preheat the oven to 350°F. Line 3 (9-inch) round cake pans with parchment paper.

2. In a large bowl, using a handheld electric mixer, beat the granulated sugar and butter for 2 minutes, or until fluffy, starting at the lowest speed and gradually increasing to the highest speed. Add the egg yolks and vanilla and beat for 3 to 4 minutes more until the mixture is fluffy, pale in color, and has tripled in volume.

3. Clean the beaters very well.

4. In another large bowl, using a handheld electric mixer, whip the egg whites for 6 to 8 minutes, starting at the lowest speed and gradually increasing to the highest speed, until you've incorporated as much air as possible and the mixture holds stiff peaks.

5. In a medium bowl, sift together the flour, cocoa powder, cornstarch, baking powder, baking soda, and salt. Add the sifted dry ingredients to the egg yolk mixture and beat for 2 minutes until smooth.

6. Use a spatula to gradually fold the egg whites into the batter. The batter should feel airy, fluffy, and have no visible streaks of egg whites remaining. Evenly divide the cake batter among the 3 prepared pans.

7. Bake the cakes for 25 to 30 minutes until puffed and spongy to the touch. Let the cakes cool in the pans.

8. Assemble the cake: Place the bottom cake layer on a cake stand or plate. Spread 1 cup of the whipped cream on the cake. Using a spoon, dollop half of the cherry filling over the whipped cream—making it even. Top that with another cake layer and repeat with another 1 cup of whipped cream and the remaining cherry filling. Add the third cake layer and top with the remaining whipped cream. Garnish with a few whole cherries.

➤ **Beyond the basics:** For an even fancier garnish, use a vegetable peeler to peel off layers from your favorite plain (not flavored) baking or eating chocolate. They will come out as chocolate curls that you can place among the cherries on top.

Raspberry Swirl Cheesecake

When you're just starting out with baking, it's perfectly fine to lean on store-bought shortcuts, such as a graham cracker piecrust. This cheesecake will still be a hit. Feel free to use mixed berries instead of raspberries here, too.

Makes 1 cake

Prep time: 20 minutes | Bake time: 50 minutes

8 ounces **cream cheese**, at room temperature

1 large **egg**

¾ cup **sugar**

1 teaspoon **vanilla extract**

⅔ cup fresh **raspberries**

1 recipe **Divine Raspberry Cheesecake Bars crust** (page 45)

2 tablespoons **raspberry jam**

1. Place an oven rack in the top middle position and preheat the oven to 350°F.

2. In a small bowl, whisk together the cream cheese, egg, sugar, and vanilla until smooth. Gently fold in the raspberries.

3. Pour the cream cheese mixture into the graham cracker piecrust.

4. Dollop the jam over the batter. Dip a knife into the dollops, and swirl the jam around—without mixing it completely into the batter.

5. Bake the cake for about 50 minutes, or until the cheesecake layer has risen to the top of the pan and does not jiggle at all when shaken. Let the cake cool for 30 minutes before serving. Or refrigerate the cake and serve it chilled!

> **Make it easier:** Forgot to take the cream cheese out of the refrigerator in time for it to reach room temperature? No problem. Simply remove the cream cheese from its wrapper, place it in a bowl, and microwave for 30 seconds to 1 minute.

Peach and Raspberry Sheet Cake

Sheet cakes are one-pan, quick-to-bake cakes that need no layering. They are great for serving a crowd and are a perfect potluck contribution. This Peach and Raspberry Sheet Cake is reminiscent of summer with bright fruity flavors in a moist yogurt-based cake.

Makes 1 cake

Prep time: 10 minutes | Bake time: 30 minutes

1½ cups **all-purpose flour**

2 teaspoons **double-acting baking powder**

Pinch **salt**

1 cup **plain Greek yogurt**

1 cup **granulated sugar**

3 large **eggs**

1 teaspoon **vanilla extract**

⅓ cup **unsalted butter**, melted

1 **peach**, pitted and thinly sliced

1 cup **raspberries**, fresh or frozen

1. Place an oven rack in the top middle position and preheat the oven to 375°F. Line a 9-by-13-inch baking pan with parchment paper. Set aside.

2. In a medium bowl, whisk the flour, baking powder, and salt until blended.

3. In a large bowl, whisk the yogurt, granulated sugar, eggs, vanilla, and melted butter until combined. Add the dry ingredients to the wet ingredients and use a handheld electric mixer to mix until just combined. Do not overmix the batter. Pour the batter into the prepared pan and spread it out.

4. Top the batter with the peach slices and raspberries in a decorative pattern, lightly pressing the fruit into the cake batter.

5. Bake the cake for about 30 minutes, or until a toothpick inserted into the center comes out clean. Let cool in the pan for 20 minutes and serve.

➤ **Beyond the basics:** Decorate this cake with a light dusting of confectioners' sugar and 2 extra peaches, thinly sliced. To really impress, arrange the peach slices in small circles to look like flowers, and then dot the center of each rose with a raspberry.

CHAPTER SEVEN

Pies

This chapter walks you through the beauty of pie making. Pies can have either an old-fashioned double crust or just a single crust with filling. Tarts, on the other hand, always only have a single crust, which is usually firmer and shorter on the sides than a piecrust, and, as such, they take less filling. Pies and tarts may be sweet or savory—both are delicious!

Keys to Baking Pie

· A good pie always starts with a good piecrust. So once you master the crust, you can play around with endless filling options. There are two types of crusts that are good for beginners: a flaky crust and a cookie-like crust. The cookie-like crust is ideal for sweet tarts because it can hold up under a watery filling. A flaky piecrust is a baking goal for many people, and, after many trials, I can tell you there's a foolproof way to achieve a perfect flaky piecrust every time.

· The secret is using grated frozen butter. Along with that frozen butter, make sure you use very cold water (to help keep the butter cold). You can either use cold water from the refrigerator or add a few ice cubes to ½ cup of water. Using frozen butter means it won't melt during the process of combining it with the flour mixture. When grated, the butter shreds are evenly dispersed throughout the dough. When the cold butter meets the hot oven, the butter's water content evaporates. This evaporation creates tiny pockets of air that make the flour rise into heavenly light and flaky layers.

· The mixing method starts with whisking the flour, sugar, and salt until combined. Add the grated frozen butter and use a fork to toss the butter shreds with the flour mixture until every piece of butter is coated well. Add the ice-cold water in small amounts— 1 tablespoon at a time is best—while using a fork to toss the dough. The dough will start to form and look like big crumbles or chunks.

· Now, press the dough with your hands. If the dough holds its shape, it's ready. Don't be tempted to add more water.

· Wrap the dough in plastic wrap and chill it. Roll the dough or press it into the pie pan when ready to use.

· Remember: The secret to a flaky crust is to bake super cold dough in a really hot oven.

Checking for Doneness

Pies are done when the crust looks golden and feels crispy to the touch. To judge when the filling is done, check to make sure it doesn't jiggle when you shake it. If you can't see the filling inside the crust, it's best to judge doneness by the color of the crust.

Fruit pies will usually bubble, so wait for the crust to be golden and the filling to be bubbling for at least 5 minutes before removing it from the oven.

Storage Guidelines

Freezing pie dough is easy, and it's the best way to prep in advance for a pie-baking session! Once the pie dough is ready, wrap it in plastic wrap and freeze it immediately for up to 3 months. Thaw the pie dough on the counter or in the refrigerator.

To prepare the pie a few days in advance, you need to prepare the pie dough and filling and refrigerate them separately. Assemble the pie or tart on baking day.

Baked pies can be kept at room temperature for up to 5 days. If, however, your pie contains dairy or egg products, it should be covered and refrigerated. You may want to freeze baked pies once they've cooled completely. Cream- or custard-based tarts are not good candidates for freezing after baking because their creamy texture changes when defrosted.

Easy Lemon-Blueberry Cobbler

This hot cobbler involves topping fruit with a batter and then dusting it with sugar before pouring hot water on top. In the oven, the water steams off, leaving a delicate, sugary crust over saucy fruit.

Makes 1 cobbler
Prep time: 15 minutes | Bake time: 50 minutes

FOR THE BERRY LAYER

2 cups fresh **blueberries**

2 teaspoons grated **lemon zest**

1 teaspoon freshly squeezed **lemon juice**

FOR THE BATTER

1 cup **all-purpose flour**

½ cup **sugar**

½ cup **milk**

3 tablespoons **unsalted butter**, melted

1 teaspoon **double-acting baking powder**

Pinch **salt**

FOR THE TOPPING

⅔ cup **sugar**

1 tablespoon **cornstarch**

¾ cup hot **water**

TO MAKE THE BERRY LAYER

1. In a 9-inch baking dish, stir together the blueberries, lemon zest, and lemon juice.

2. Spread the berries into an even layer.

TO MAKE THE BATTER

1. Place an oven rack in the top middle position and preheat the oven to 375°F.

2. In a small bowl, combine the flour, sugar, milk, melted butter, baking powder, and salt. Using a fork, mix well. Avoid overmixing the batter.

3. Use a spatula to spread the cobbler dough over the berries as well as you can. It doesn't have to be perfect.

1. In another small bowl, whisk the sugar and cornstarch until blended. Sprinkle the sugar mixture over the batter—don't mix it in.

2. Slowly and evenly pour the hot water over the sugar layer.

3. Bake the cobbler for 50 minutes, or until golden. Enjoy the cobbler warm or cold.

▷ **Swap it:** Any type of berry works here—the same amount of blackberries is a great alternative. Orange zest makes a great substitute for lemon zest, too.

Mini Apple Pies

We don't always have the time to wait for a large pie to bake, so I often make these Mini Apple Pies in a 12-cup muffin pan. They bake in 20 minutes and are just as satisfying as the larger version!

Makes 12 mini pies
Prep time: 30 minutes | Chill time: 30 minutes | Bake time: 20 minutes

FOR THE CRUST

2½ cups **all-purpose flour**

¼ cup **sugar**

½ teaspoon **salt**

1 cup **unsalted butter**, frozen

3 to 5 tablespoons ice **water**

FOR THE FILLING

4 large **apples**, peeled and cut into ¼-inch pieces

1 cup **sugar**

6 tablespoons **all-purpose flour**

3 tablespoons **unsalted butter**, at room temperature

2 teaspoons ground **cinnamon**

TO MAKE THE CRUST

1. In a large bowl, whisk the flour, sugar, and salt until well blended.

2. Using a box grater, grate the frozen butter into the flour mixture. Using a fork, toss the flour and butter until the flour evenly coats the butter. Add the ice-cold water a little at a time, and keep tossing with the fork until the dough comes together. It will look like a big crumbly mess. Squeeze the dough with your hand; if it holds its shape, it's ready. Divide the dough in half and wrap each half with plastic. Refrigerate the dough for at least 30 minutes, and up to 1 week.

TO MAKE THE FILLING

1. Place an oven rack in the top middle position and preheat the oven to 425°F.

2. In a medium bowl, combine the apples, sugar, flour, butter, and cinnamon. Using a spatula, mix well.

3. Lightly dust a work surface with flour and place the dough on it. Roll each half of the dough into a 12-inch circle about ⅛-inch thick. Using a 4-inch round cutter, cut out circles from both halves. Reroll the scraps and cut more circles, as needed, to get a total of 12.

4. Butter the cups of a 12-cup muffin pan. Place each mini piecrust into the bottom of each muffin cup, pushing it down and up the sides to cover.

5. Place 2 or 3 tablespoons of filling into each piecrust.

6. Bake for 18 to 20 minutes until golden.

➤ **Swap it:** Use 1 tablespoon of orange zest and $1/3$ cup of dried cranberries in the filling instead of the cinnamon for a festive holiday flavor.

Fruit Streusel Pie

This dessert is the perfect combination of pie and crumble, all drenched with juicy fruit. Make yours with peaches, blueberries, strawberries, or apples—or a combination of fruits and berries—they all work!

Makes 1 pie
Prep time: 20 minutes | Bake time: 50 minutes

FOR THE CRUST

2½ cups **all-purpose flour**

½ cup **sugar**, divided

½ teaspoon **salt**

1 cup **unsalted butter**, frozen

5 tablespoons ice **water,** divided

FOR THE FILLING

4 cups fresh **fruit**, sliced or diced

¾ cup **sugar**

4 tablespoons **cornstarch**

1 teaspoon **vanilla extract**

Pinch **salt**

TO MAKE THE CRUST

1. In a large bowl, whisk the flour, ¼ cup of sugar, and salt until blended. Using a box grater, grate the frozen butter into the flour mixture. Use a fork to toss the flour and butter until the flour evenly coats the butter. Remove 1¼ cups of the crust mixture and set it aside.

2. To the remaining crust mixture, add 2 tablespoons of ice-cold water and toss with a fork. You can add up to a total of 4 tablespoons of ice-cold water until the dough comes together. It will look like a big crumbly mess.

3. Squeeze the dough with your hand; if it holds its shape, it's ready. Press the crust into the bottom and up the sides of a pie pan. Refrigerate the crust until ready to bake.

TO MAKE THE FILLING

1. To the reserved crust mixture, add the remaining ¼ cup of sugar and remaining 1 tablespoon of ice-cold water and toss well with a fork until it forms a crumble. This mixture should not feel like pie dough, so it won't hold its shape. Set streusel aside.

CONTINUED

2. Place an oven rack in the top middle position and preheat the oven to 425°F.

3. In a large bowl, using a spoon, toss the fruit, sugar, cornstarch, vanilla, and salt to combine.

4. Remove the crust from the refrigerator and spread the fruit filling over it as evenly as you can. Scatter the streusel over the fruit, and gently press it down with your hands.

5. Bake the pie for 20 minutes. Reduce the oven temperature to 350°F. Bake the pie for 25 to 30 minutes more, until the crust and topping are golden and the filling is bubbling. Let cool for 20 minutes before serving. Serve with ice cream or as is.

➤ **Make it easier:** Using the same pie dough base to make both piecrust and streusel is a great time-saver. Make sure to remove the 1¼ cups of the crust mixture before adding the water to make the dough. When adding the water to make the streusel, make sure the crumble doesn't hold its shape like pie dough.

Lemon Tart

This is a bright, fresh, summer favorite. Unlike most tarts or pies, this recipe relies on baking the crust fully before you fill it. The filling requires no baking—just a light bit of stovetop cooking.

Makes 1 tart
Prep time: 15 minutes | Bake time: 35 minutes | Cook time: 10 minutes
Chill time: 2 hours

FOR THE CRUST

1 cup **all-purpose flour**
½ cup finely crushed **almonds**
¼ cup **granulated sugar**
Pinch **salt**
½ cup **unsalted butter**, frozen
3 to 4 tablespoons ice **water**

FOR THE FILLING

3 cups **heavy (whipping) cream**
½ cup **granulated sugar**
2 tablespoons grated **lemon zest**
¼ cup **lemon juice**
1 tablespoon **unsalted butter**
2 teaspoons **vanilla extract**
Pinch **salt**

TO MAKE THE CRUST

1. Place an oven rack in the top middle position and preheat the oven to 400°F.

2. In a large bowl, whisk the flour, almonds, granulated sugar, and salt until blended. Using a box grater, grate the frozen butter into the flour mixture. Use a fork to toss the flour and butter. Add the water a little at a time, and keep tossing until the dough comes together. Squeeze the dough with your hand. If it holds its shape, it's ready. Press the dough into a 9-inch tart pan, covering the bottom and sides.

3. Bake the crust for 35 minutes, or until golden and firm to the touch. Let cool for 30 minutes before adding the filling.

TO MAKE THE FILLING

1. In a 3-quart saucepan over medium heat, combine the heavy cream and granulated sugar. Cover the saucepan and bring the mixture to a boil. Add the lemon zest. Let the mixture boil for 7 minutes and turn off the heat.

CONTINUED

Lemon Tart continued

2. Add the lemon juice, butter, vanilla, and salt, whisking to combine. Refrigerate the filling for 10 minutes.

3. Pour the cooled filling over the crust. Chill the tart for 1 to 2 hours until the filling has set.

➤ **Beyond the basics:** Top the tart with whole cranberry sauce for a spectacular holiday dessert!

French Pear Custard Tart

This recipe is derived from a classic French pastry. It is rich and silky smooth with a sweet crust patted right into the tart pan—no need for chilling or rolling the dough.

Makes 1 tart
Prep time: 15 minutes | Bake time: 45 minutes

FOR THE CRUST

1¼ cups **all-purpose flour**

½ cup **sugar**

Pinch **salt**

½ cup **unsalted butter**, frozen

2 to 3 tablespoons ice **water**

FOR THE FILLING

3 **pears**, peeled, cored, and thinly sliced

⅓ cup **sugar**

¼ cup **all-purpose flour**

2 large **eggs**

¾ cup **heavy (whipping) cream**

1 teaspoon **vanilla extract**

TO MAKE THE CRUST

1. Place an oven rack in the top middle position and preheat the oven to 375°F.

2. In a large bowl, whisk the flour, sugar, and salt until blended. Using a box grater, grate the frozen butter into the flour mixture. Using a fork, toss the flour and butter until the flour evenly coats the butter. Add the water a little at a time, and keep tossing the mixture with the fork until the dough comes together. Squeeze the dough with your hand. If it holds its shape, it's ready. Put the dough into the tart pan and press it into the bottom and up the sides of the pan.

TO MAKE THE FILLING

1. Arrange the pear slices over the crust.

2. In a medium bowl, whisk the sugar, flour, eggs, heavy cream, and vanilla until blended. Pour the filling over the pears. Place the tart pan on a baking sheet.

3. Bake the tart for 35 to 45 minutes, or until the filling has set. Let cool before serving.

➤ **Make it easier:** Peeling the pears is optional here. If you're pressed for time, feel free to leave the peels on.

Peach Hand Pies

These super easy individual peach pies are made to fit in your hand. Sweet, juicy peaches are tossed with sugar and butter and wrapped in a golden crust. Satisfying and comforting, these are done in one-third the time of a regular pie!

Makes 6 hand pies

Prep time: 30 minutes | Bake time: 40 minutes

3 large **peaches**, pitted and cut into ½-inch cubes

½ cup **sugar**

2 tablespoons **all-purpose flour**

1 teaspoon freshly squeezed **lemon juice**

½ recipe **Mini Apple Pies crust** (page 114)

All-purpose flour, for the work surface

1 large **egg**

1 tablespoon **heavy (whipping) cream**

1. In a medium bowl, use a spatula to combine the peaches, sugar, flour, and lemon juice.

2. Place an oven rack in the top middle position and preheat the oven to 420°F. Line a baking sheet with parchment paper.

3. Lightly dust a work surface with flour and place the dough on it. Roll out the dough into a 12-inch circle about ⅛-inch thick. Using a 4-inch round cookie cutter, cut 6 circles from the dough, rerolling the scraps and cutting more circles, if needed.

4. Evenly divide the filling among the circles. Try to keep the filling on the top half of the circles. Fold the bottom half of the circle over the filling to meet the upper half. Use a fork to seal the edges.

5. In a small bowl, whisk the egg and cream to make an egg wash. Using a pastry brush, brush the egg wash over the piecrusts.

6. Place the hand pies on a baking sheet and bake for 35 to 40 minutes, or until the crust is golden.

➤ Swap it: In cherry season, swap 2½ cups of pitted fresh cherries for the peaches.

Mushroom and Spinach Quiche

There are two steps to a successful quiche: Bake the crust halfway before filling for a crispy final crust, and cook the fillings before adding them to the crust for baking. This mushroom and spinach combination is a classic.

Makes 1 quiche
Prep time: 15 minutes | Cook time: 12 minutes | Bake time: 1 hour

FOR THE CRUST

1¼ cups **all-purpose flour**

1 tablespoon **sugar**

1 teaspoon **salt**

1 tablespoon chopped fresh **thyme** leaves

½ cup **unsalted butter**, frozen

2 to 4 tablespoons ice **water**

FOR THE FILLING

2 cups **light cream** (or half-and-half)

2 large **eggs**

½ cup shredded **Parmesan cheese**

1 teaspoon **salt**

1 teaspoon freshly ground **black pepper**

1 tablespoon minced fresh **thyme** leaves

1 tablespoon **all-purpose flour**

1 tablespoon **unsalted butter**

2 **garlic cloves**, minced

1 cup sliced **mushrooms**

2 cups fresh **spinach** leaves

TO MAKE THE CRUST

1. Place an oven rack in the top middle position and preheat the oven to 430°F.

2. In a large bowl, whisk the flour, sugar, salt, and thyme until blended. Using a box grater, grate the frozen butter into the flour mixture. Using a fork, toss the flour and butter until the flour evenly coats the butter. Add the ice-cold water a little at a time, and keep tossing the mixture with a fork until the dough comes together. It will look like a big crumbly mess. Squeeze the dough with your hand. If it holds its shape, it's ready. Press the dough into a 9-inch tart pan, covering the bottom and sides. Prick the dough all over with a fork.

3. Bake the crust for 20 minutes, or until firm and slightly tan in color.

TO MAKE THE FILLING

1. While the crust bakes, in a large bowl, combine the cream, eggs, Parmesan cheese, salt, pepper, thyme, and flour. Whisk until smooth and well blended.

2. In a medium nonstick skillet over medium-high heat, melt the butter. Add the garlic and sauté for 2 minutes until fragrant and opaque.

3. Add the mushrooms and sauté for 4 minutes until cooked. Add the spinach and sauté for 4 to 5 minutes until no more water or liquid is released from the spinach. Using a slotted spoon, transfer the mushroom and spinach mixture (leaving any excess liquid in the pan) to the cream and eggs mixture. Stir well to combine. Pour the filling over the crust.

4. Reduce the oven temperature to 350°F.

5. Bake the quiche for 30 to 40 minutes, or until the filling has set. Let cool for 15 to 20 minutes before slicing and serving.

➤ **Swap it:** Customize the filling with 1 cup of chopped roasted bell peppers, 1 cup of cooked ground beef, 1 cup of chopped roasted asparagus, or 1 cup of shredded roasted chicken. Feel free to experiment with any combo of meats, veggies, and cheeses you like.

Honey Pecan Crunch Pie

I never appreciated pecan pie until I made this Honey Pecan Crunch Pie. There's something about the honey flavor that pairs beautifully with pecans, butter, vanilla, and brown sugar in a piecrust.

Makes 1 pie

Prep time: 30 minutes | Cook time: 5 minutes | Bake time: 1 hour 10 minutes

FOR THE CRUST

1¼ cups **all-purpose flour**, plus more for the work surface

¼ cup **sugar**

Pinch **salt**

½ cup **unsalted butter**, frozen

2 to 3 tablespoons ice **water**

FOR THE FILLING

2 cups **pecan halves**

½ cup **unsalted butter**

1 cup packed **light brown sugar**

½ cup **honey**

Pinch **salt**

2 teaspoons **vanilla extract**

2 large **eggs**

TO MAKE THE CRUST

1. Place an oven rack in the top middle position and preheat the oven to 425°F.

2. In a large bowl, whisk the flour, sugar, and salt until blended. Using a box grater, grate the frozen butter into the flour mixture. Using a fork, toss the flour and butter until the flour evenly coats the butter. Add the ice-cold water a little at a time, and keep tossing the mixture with the fork until the dough comes together. It will look like a big crumbly mess. Squeeze the dough with your hand. If it holds its shape, it's ready.

3. Lightly flour a work surface and place the dough on it. Roll the dough to fit a 9-inch pie pan. Place the dough into the pan, covering the bottom and sides. Prick the dough all over with a fork.

4. Bake the pie without any filling—this is called blind-baking—for 15 to 18 minutes until it has firmed up but is not yet golden in color. Remove and let cool.

CONTINUED

Honey Pecan Crunch Pie CONTINUED

TO MAKE THE FILLING

1. Starting in the center of the cooled crust, arrange the pecan halves in concentric circles until they cover the bottom of the crust.

2. In a 2-quart saucepan over medium heat, melt the butter. Whisk in the brown sugar, honey, and salt. Cook the mixture for 2 minutes until everything is dissolved and well blended. Remove the pan from the heat and whisk in the vanilla and the eggs. Carefully pour the filling over the pecans in the crust.

3. Reduce the oven temperature to 375°F.

4. Bake the pie for 40 to 50 minutes until the filling has set. Let cool for 20 minutes before slicing and serving.

▷ **Pro tip:** Wash your hands in very cold water before handling pie dough to keep the dough chilled; you don't want the dough to be compromised by your own body heat.

CHAPTER EIGHT

Yeast Breads

It's time to dive into the deliciously soft, chewy, and oh-so-satisfying world of yeast breads. This category is vast and can vary from easy, straightforward recipes to long hours of prep and complicated formulas. We'll focus on straightforward, foolproof versions of yeast breads, learning about yeast and how to work with it.

Keys to Baking Bread

· When making yeast bread, remember to plan ahead. That's because yeast requires time to activate and reach its full working capacity. Also, for most recipes, the dough needs time to rest and relax in order to be shaped. Usually, a good rule of thumb is to plan for about 3 hours. You won't be actively working during all this time, but you will be waiting to proceed to the next step. Most recipes can be made the night before baking, if that's more convenient for you.

· Yeast is what causes your breads to rise. Once yeast is activated it starts to slowly release gases that stretch the structure of the dough. You can activate yeast by feeding it sugar at room temperature and combining it with a warm (about 100°F) liquid. As the yeast consumes the sugar and begins to release gas, the mixture bubbles or foams a bit. That's an indication the yeast is active.

◀ PRETZEL STICKS (PAGE 136)

- Yeast comes in two forms: fresh yeast (also known as cake yeast) and dry yeast. Fresh yeast is highly perishable and isn't for the home baker. In all of my recipes I use a type of dry yeast called instant yeast, also known as rapid-rise yeast. The other type of dry yeast is regular, or active dry, yeast.

- The benefit of using instant yeast versus regular yeast is the speed of action. Instant yeast acts faster and requires only one full proof.

- Allowing the dough to rest for at least 1 to 1½ hours at room temperature helps the dough ferment and enriches the flavor of your yeast breads. Finally, during baking, the yeast continues to release more gas, expanding the dough, and forming its structure.

- Kneading dough is a process that activates the flour proteins to create a stretchy, chewy texture. You need to knead the dough right after it is mixed. Kneading by hand usually takes 7 to 8 minutes.

- The best way to knead dough is on a lightly floured surface, but be careful about using too much flour for this step. The amount of flour needed will vary based on the type of flour used in the recipe, the humidity of your kitchen, or the general dryness of the climate. Adding too much flour will result in tough, dry bread. Know that as you knead the dough, the flour will gradually hydrate. As this happens, you won't feel the wetness, or the need to add extra flour. Patience is key, and knowing that gradually, as you knead, the dough will come together.

- To knead dough properly, form the dough into a ball on the floured surface and push it down with both hands, one on top of the other, using just the heel of one hand. Rotate the dough a half turn and repeat the process. Keep rotating and pushing down on the dough until it starts to feel smooth and elastic.

- At that point, the dough will be impossible to shape, so it is "proofed." This means you set the dough aside, covered, to rest and relax for 1 to 1½ hours. This rest time allows the yeast to expand more and the dough to become malleable again for shaping.

- The shaping process is next and the second "proof" happens, usually for about 30 minutes, after shaping. Then baking begins.

Checking for Doneness

Yeast breads are done when they have fully expanded and hold their shape. Once the bread is hard to the touch and has a golden color, it is done. As with most other baked goods, the toothpick test can help determine doneness—when one is inserted into the bread's center and comes out clean, the bread is done.

Be careful with egg- and milk-rich breads—they brown quickly, which can be a false indication of their doneness. These breads brown quickly because of their high sugar content, which caramelizes and lends to the brown color, and the protein in the eggs. It's best to cover these breads with aluminum foil once they've reached a golden color. You can continue baking the bread, covered, until the insides have cooked through.

Storage Guidelines

Once baked and cooled, yeast breads can be wrapped and frozen for up to 6 months. To thaw frozen baked breads, place them on the counter at room temperature for 2 to 4 hours. You may rewarm the bread in a 350°F oven for 5 minutes, if you wish.

Freezing unbaked bread dough is another great way to prepare yeast breads in advance. You'll prepare the dough as instructed, knead it, and then freeze it right away—without proofing. When you are ready to bake the bread, remove the dough from the freezer and thaw it on the counter. This will count as the first proof. Then you'll need to shape it and proof it a second time. Then continue the baking process.

Pretzel Sticks

Pretzels are a perennial favorite treat. They remind me of Vienna, where you can have pretzels plain, stuffed, dipped—you name it! Pretzels offer two unique features: a deep flavor unlike any other bread and a chewy texture.

Makes 16 sticks

Prep time: 45 minutes | Rest time: 1 hour 30 minutes | Cook time: 8 minutes

Bake time: 18 minutes

1½ cups warm (100°F) **water**

2 tablespoons **sugar**

2 teaspoons **instant yeast** (or rapid-rise yeast)

4½ cups **all-purpose flour**, divided

2 teaspoons **salt**

4 tablespoons **unsalted butter**, melted

Light **olive oil**

5 cups, plus 1 teaspoon **water**

¼ cup **baking soda**

1 large **egg**

Coarse **salt**, for garnish (optional)

1. Line 2 baking sheets with parchment paper.

2. In a large glass measuring cup, combine the warm water, sugar, and yeast. Using a fork, blend until well combined. Set aside for 3 minutes to activate the yeast.

3. In a large bowl, whisk 4 cups of flour and the salt until blended.

4. Stir the melted butter into the yeast mixture. Add the yeast mixture to the flour mixture and knead the dough with clean hands for 7 to 8 minutes until smooth and malleable, adding up to the remaining ½ cup of flour, as needed.

5. Coat another large bowl with olive oil. Place the dough in the bowl. Cover the bowl with plastic wrap and place it in a warm, dry place to sit for 1½ hours until the dough has nearly tripled in volume.

6. Remove the dough from the bowl and divide it into 2 pieces. Cut each piece into 8 smaller pieces, for 16 pieces total. Roll each piece into a rope about 5 inches long. Place the ropes on the prepared baking sheets, and preheat the oven to 425°F.

7. In a 4-quart pot over high heat, combine the 5 cups of water and the baking soda. Bring to a boil.

8. Using tongs, place one pretzel stick at a time into the boiling water for 30 seconds. You'll see the pretzels puff a bit. This boiling process is crucial for the chewy texture, crackly appearance, and beloved pretzel flavor. Using a slotted spoon, remove the pretzel and place it back on the baking sheet. The pretzel will start to wrinkle or shrink on the surface—that's okay. Boil each remaining pretzel stick in the same way.

9. In a small bowl, whisk the egg and remaining 1 teaspoon of water until blended. Using a pastry brush, brush the surface of each pretzel with the egg wash. Sprinkle the coarse salt over the pretzels (if using).

10. Bake the pretzels for 15 to 18 minutes, switching the baking sheets two-thirds of the way through the baking time, until deep golden in color. Let cool for 15 minutes before serving.

➤ Swap it: Instead of topping these pretzels with the classic coarse salt crystals, try sprinkling poppy seeds or sesame seeds over them before baking.

Foolproof Dinner Rolls

This is a perfect recipe to start your yeast bread–baking experience. I love this basic soft dough because of its balance of chewy texture and tender bite.

Makes 24 rolls

Prep time: 30 minutes | Rest time: 2 hours | Bake time: 30 minutes

2½ cups **all-purpose flour**, plus more as needed

1½ teaspoons **kosher salt**

1 cup warm (100°F) **water**

3 tablespoons **sugar**

2 teaspoons **instant yeast**

2 tablespoons **unsalted butter**, melted

1 large **egg**

Light **olive oil**

1. In a large mixing bowl, whisk the flour and salt.

2. In a large glass measuring cup, stir together the warm water, sugar, and yeast. Let sit for 2 to 3 minutes until the yeast starts to activate—the mixture will turn cloudy and may foam on top.

3. Add the melted butter and egg to the yeast mixture. Stir well to combine. Pour the yeast mixture into the flour mixture and knead the dough by hand for 4 to 6 minutes until smooth and just a bit sticky when you press your finger deep into the dough. Add a little extra flour, up to ¼ cup, if the dough still feels too sticky, but resist adding too much or the dough will become too dry. Coat a large bowl with a little olive oil and place the bread dough in it. Cover it with plastic wrap and set aside in a warm, dry place and let the dough rise until it doubles in size (1 to 2 hours).

4. Place an oven rack in the middle position and preheat the oven to 350°F. Line a baking sheet with parchment paper.

5. Dust a work surface and rolling pin with flour. Divide the dough into 4 pieces. Roll each piece into a long rope and cut off 2-inch-long pieces. Roll each piece into a ball about 1½ inches in diameter. Place the dough balls on the prepared baking sheet. Cover the baking sheet with plastic wrap and let rest for 30 minutes before baking.

6. Bake the rolls for 30 minutes, until golden.

➤ **Swap it:** Make whole-wheat dinner rolls: Replace the all-purpose flour with 2 1/4 cups whole-wheat flour and proceed with the recipe.

Challah

Challah dough is usually braided, making it a showstopper on any brunch or dinner table. Because of the high butter and egg content in challah dough, you'll notice that it doesn't rise as much as other yeast bread doughs. This is normal.

Makes 1 loaf
Prep time: 30 minutes | Rest time: 2 hours | Bake time: 40 minutes

¼ cup warm (100°F) **water**

2 tablespoons **honey**

2 tablespoons **sugar**

2 teaspoons **instant yeast** (or rapid-rise yeast)

½ cup **milk**

4 tablespoons **unsalted butter**, at room temperature

3 large **eggs**, divided

3½ cups **all-purpose flour**, plus more as needed

1 teaspoon **salt**

Light **olive oil**

1. In a small bowl, whisk the warm water, honey, sugar, and yeast until blended. Set aside for about 2 minutes to let the yeast activate (it will bubble).

2. In a large glass measuring cup, combine the milk and butter. Microwave for 2 minutes until the milk is warm and the butter melts. Transfer the mixture to a large bowl. Add 2 eggs and mix well until blended. Add the yeast mixture to the milk and egg mixture and whisk to combine.

3. In a large bowl, whisk the flour and salt until blended. Slowly stir the flour mixture into the wet ingredients to form the dough. Knead the dough by hand for 7 to 8 minutes until the dough feels soft and elastic. Don't add more flour; it will dry out the dough.

4. Coat another large bowl with a little olive oil. Place the dough in the bowl. Cover the bowl with plastic wrap and place it in a warm, dry place to proof for 1½ to 2 hours, until it doubles in size.

5. Turn the dough out onto a work surface. Avoid using additional flour here. Divide the dough into 3 equal parts. Roll each part into a 12- to 14-inch-long strand.

CONTINUED

6. Join the 3 dough strands at the top by pressing them together tightly. Lay the joined strands on a work surface and braid them into a loose braid; avoid stretching the dough too hard or pulling it out while braiding. Press the bottom of the braid together as you did the top part to join the strands. Place the braid on a baking sheet and cover it with plastic. Let it rest again for 30 minutes.

7. Place an oven rack in the top middle position and preheat the oven to 350°F. Just before baking, in a small bowl, whisk the remaining egg and 1 tablespoon of water until blended. Evenly brush the challah with the egg wash.

8. Bake the challah for 35 to 40 minutes until golden and cooked through. It should produce a hollow sound when tapped. Remove from the oven and let cool for 30 minutes before serving.

➤ **Pro tip:** As you braid the challah, you'll notice the loaf's ends are thinner than the middle, which can result in burnt edges. To prevent this, tuck under about $1\frac{1}{2}$ inches of dough at each end so the whole loaf will have a similar thickness. It will bake evenly and look beautiful.

No-Knead Olive-Walnut Bread

For many beginners, overnight breads are a bit easier to make and their rustic appearance seems less fussy.

Makes 1 loaf
Prep time: 20 minutes | Rest time: 12 hours | Bake time: 50 minutes

3½ cups **all-purpose flour**, plus more for the work surface

1 teaspoon **salt**

½ teaspoon **instant yeast** (or rapid-rise yeast)

1⅔ cups warm (100°F) **water**

1 cup pitted **black olives**, drained and roughly chopped

⅔ cups **walnuts**, roughly chopped

1. In a large bowl, using a spatula, mix the flour, salt, and yeast. Add the warm water and continue to mix. The dough will be messy, sticky, and clumpy. Cover the dough and let sit overnight, or up to 12 hours.

2. The next morning, using a spatula, mix in the olives and walnuts. Lightly flour a work surface and turn the dough out onto it. Shape the dough into a circle. Don't worry about perfection; this is a rustic bread.

3. Place an oven rack in the top middle position and preheat the oven to 420°F. Line a baking sheet with parchment paper.

4. Transfer the loaf to the prepared baking sheet. Cover the dough and let sit for 30 minutes. Because the dough is sticky, expect it to deflate into a flat round or oval shape as it proofs, and even during baking. That's okay.

5. Bake the bread on the baking sheet for 30 minutes. Reduce the oven temperature to 375°F and bake the bread for 15 to 20 minutes more until the color is golden and it sounds hollow when tapped. Let cool for 1 hour before slicing.

➤ Swap it: This bread is easy to customize. Instead of the olive-walnut combination, try adding ½ cup of feta cheese with 1 cup of sun-dried tomatoes, or ½ cup of dried fruit, such as figs or apricots, with 1 cup of cheddar cheese and 2 tablespoons of thyme.

Best Cinnamon Rolls

Cinnamon rolls are the key to my heart. In this recipe, you'll cream the sugar and butter as if making a cake. This little tweak creates an unbeatable fluffy texture!

Makes 12 rolls

Prep time: 30 minutes | Rest time: 3 hours | Bake time: 20 minutes

FOR THE DOUGH

½ cup warm (100°F) **water**

¼ cup, plus 2 tablespoons **granulated sugar**

2 teaspoons **instant yeast**

6 tablespoons **unsalted butter**, at room temperature

1 large **egg**

½ cup warm (100°F) **milk**

3 to 3½ cups **all-purpose flour**, plus more for the work surface

1½ teaspoons **salt**

Light **olive oil**

FOR THE FILLING

2 tablespoons ground **cinnamon**

1 cup packed **light brown sugar**

4 tablespoons **unsalted butter**, melted

TO MAKE THE DOUGH

1. Using a fork, stir together the water, 2 tablespoons of granulated sugar, and the yeast. Set aside to activate the yeast.

2. In a large bowl, using a handheld electric mixer, beat the butter and remaining ¼ cup of granulated sugar for 3 minutes, or until fluffy, starting on the lowest speed and gradually increasing to the highest speed. Add the egg and beat for 2 minutes more. Add the warm milk and beat for 1 minute until the mixture is well blended.

3. Add the yeast mixture to the butter mixture and whisk it in.

4. Add 3 cups of flour and the salt. Using clean hands, knead the dough for about 7 minutes until the dough is smooth and elastic, adding up to the remaining ½ cup of flour, as needed.

5. Coat another large bowl with a little olive oil. Place the dough in the bowl. Cover the bowl with plastic wrap and place it in a warm, dry place to sit for 2 hours until the dough is doubled in size.

CONTINUED

Best Cinnamon Rolls

TO MAKE THE FILLING

1. In a small bowl, whisk the cinnamon and brown sugar until combined.

2. Lightly flour a work surface and place the dough on it. Roll the dough into a large rectangle about ⅛-inch thick, with the long sides of the rectangle parallel to you. Brush the entire surface of the rectangle with butter, leaving a 1-inch border at the longest sides. Sprinkle the filling over the entire buttered surface. Starting with a long side of the rectangle closest to you, roll the dough over the sugar topping to form a cylinder.

3. Using a sharp knife, cut 1-inch pieces along the length of the cylinder. Place the rolls on the baking sheet about 1 inch apart. Cover the rolls with plastic wrap and let them rise again for 1 hour.

4. Place an oven rack in the top middle position and preheat the oven to 375°F.

5. Bake the cinnamon rolls for 18 to 20 minutes until they are slightly golden on the edges.

➤ **Beyond the basics:** To take these up a notch, top the rolls with a glaze while they are still warm after baking. To make the glaze: In a medium bowl, whisk 1 cup of confectioners' sugar, 4 ounces of room-temperature cream cheese, 3 tablespoons of milk, and 1 teaspoon of vanilla extract until smooth. Adjust the consistency by adding more milk, a little at a time, for a thinner glaze, or more confectioners' sugar for a thicker glaze.

Easy Garlic Parmesan Knots

These garlic Parmesan knots are soft, fluffy, and savory. Enjoy these on the table with dinner, or use them as buns for sliders!

Makes 20 knots

Prep time: 30 minutes | Rest time: 2 hours | Bake time: 20 minutes

FOR THE KNOTS

2¾ cups **all-purpose flour**, divided

1 teaspoon **garlic powder**

1½ teaspoons **kosher salt**

1 cup warm **water** (100°F)

3 tablespoons **sugar**

2 teaspoons **instant yeast**

2 tablespoons **unsalted butter**, melted

1 large **egg**

½ cup grated **Parmesan cheese**

Light **olive oil**

FOR THE GARLIC BUTTER

5 tablespoons plus 1 teaspoon **unsalted butter**, melted

¼ cup grated **Parmesan cheese**

2 tablespoons fresh minced **herbs**

2 **garlic cloves**, minced

½ teaspoon **kosher salt**

TO MAKE THE KNOTS

1. In a large bowl, whisk 2½ cups of flour, the garlic powder, and salt to combine.

2. In a large glass measuring cup, stir together the water, sugar, and yeast. Let sit for 2 to 3 minutes until the yeast starts to activate—the mixture will turn cloudy and may foam on top.

3. Add the melted butter and egg to the yeast mixture. Stir well to combine.

4. Using a fork, stir in the Parmesan cheese. Pour the yeast mixture into the flour mixture and begin kneading the dough by hand for 4 to 6 minutes until smooth and just a bit sticky when you press your finger deep into the dough. Add a little extra flour, up to the remaining ¼ cup, if the dough still feels too sticky, but resist adding too much or the dough will become too dry.

5. Coat another large bowl with olive oil. Place the dough in the bowl. Cover the bowl with plastic wrap and place it in a warm, dry place to sit until the dough doubles in size. This may take 1 to 2 hours depending on how warm your home is.

CONTINUED

Easy Garlic Parmesan Knots CONTINUED

6. Place an oven rack in the middle position and preheat the oven to 350°F. Line 2 baking sheets with parchment paper.

7. While the oven is preheating, shape your dough. Divide the dough into 4 pieces. Roll each piece into a 20-inch-long rope. Using a sharp knife, cut the ropes into 4-inch pieces. Tie each piece into a loose knot and place the knots on the prepared baking sheets. Cover the baking sheets with plastic wrap and let the knots rest for another 30 minutes.

TO MAKE THE GARLIC BUTTER

1. In a small bowl, using a fork, stir together the melted butter, Parmesan cheese, herbs, garlic, and salt. Using a pastry brush, brush the tops of the knots with half of the garlic butter.

2. Bake the knots for 18 to 20 minutes, switching the baking sheets two-thirds of the way through the baking time, until golden.

3. As soon as the knots come out of the oven, brush them with the remaining garlic butter. Let cool for 15 minutes before serving.

➤ **Pro tip:** Brushing the knots both before and after baking infuses them with so much flavor! Be careful when shaping the knots—do not leave any tips of dough protruding, as they will burn. To prevent this, you have two options: Either make a very loose knot so the tips barely protrude, or tuck the tips under the knot.

Making More or Less

The best thing about baking is how easy it is to double, triple, or even quadruple a recipe, so you don't have to start from scratch to make your delicious treats for a crowd. Just take one ingredient at a time and multiply the amount by two, three, or four (or more). Make sure you repeat the same procedure with all the remaining ingredients. Have all the necessary pans prepped, and proceed with the recipe as written.

If you're baking for just two people, or even just one person, and would like to halve a recipe, it's best to bake the full recipe amount and freeze the leftovers according to the storage guidelines. However, in some cases you can divide the flour, sugar, butter, and other ingredients easily by half. Pay attention to the egg—it's challenging to divide it in half. The best way to do so is to crack an egg into a bowl, whisk it well and measure out how many tablespoons you have, then measure the amount you need by tablespoons.

Measurement Conversions

VOLUME EQUIVALENTS (LIQUID)

US Standard	US Standard (ounces)	Metric (approximate)
2 tablespoons	1 fl. oz.	30 mL
¼ cup	2 fl. oz.	60 mL
½ cup	4 fl. oz.	120 mL
1 cup	8 fl. oz.	240 mL
1½ cups	12 fl. oz.	355 mL
2 cups or 1 pint	16 fl. oz.	475 mL
4 cups or 1 quart	32 fl. oz.	1 L
1 gallon	128 fl. oz.	4 L

OVEN TEMPERATURES

Fahrenheit (F)	Celsius (C) (approximate)
250°F	120°C
300°F	150°C
325°F	165°C
350°F	180°C
375°F	190°C
400°F	200°C
425°F	220°C
450°F	230°C

VOLUME EQUIVALENTS (DRY)

US Standard	Metric (approximate)
⅛ teaspoon	0.5 mL
¼ teaspoon	1 mL
½ teaspoon	2 mL
¾ teaspoon	4 mL
1 teaspoon	5 mL
1 tablespoon	15 mL
¼ cup	59 mL
⅓ cup	79 mL
½ cup	118 mL
⅔ cup	156 mL
¾ cup	177 mL
1 cup	235 mL
2 cups or 1 pint	475 mL
3 cups	700 mL
4 cups or 1 quart	1 L

WEIGHT EQUIVALENTS

US Standard	Metric (approximate)
½ ounce	15 g
1 ounce	30 g
2 ounces	60 g
4 ounces	115 g
8 ounces	225 g
12 ounces	340 g
16 ounces or 1 pound	455 g

Index

Acknowledgments

Thank you to Callisto Media and the wonderful team of editors I worked with who helped me reach this goal. I'm forever grateful to you!

To my family, who've shown me the world and all its different cultures and flavors, and who've pushed me to experience it.

To my husband, who's my home, my comfort, and my never-ending support. You've tried thousands of recipes throughout the years and you've never complained—even when I was still learning and the results were far from perfect.

To my girls, Dania and Jana, who challenge and reward me every single minute of the day. I love you. You've been busy baking with me and you've made the recipes extra fun, extra messy, and extra delicious!

To my friends, who've tasted my baked goods, tested some of the recipes, and inspired me to keep going.

About the Author

Mahy Elamin is a busy mom, culinary instructor, and food blogger at *Two Purple Figs*. A former pharmacist who couldn't stop dreaming about being in the kitchen to create something new and delicious, she finally pulled the plug on her job and decided to dive into the world of food and food science—and never looked back. She loves simplifying things in the kitchen using her science background and experience. Mahy has lived in 12 different countries, so many of her recipes are a fusion of flavors and techniques from around the world. She has two girls, Dania and Jana, who are her most valuable kitchen helpers.

CPSIA information can be obtained
at www.ICGtesting.com
Printed in the USA
BVHW090720250420
578248BV00013B/622